Leaders Everywhere!

Nurturing a Leadership Culture in Your Organization

Expanded Edition

By

Dr. Tim Elmore

&

Dr. Art Fuller

Published by Growing Leaders, Inc.

3550 Corporate Way / Suite C
Duluth, GA 30096
(770) 495-3332

www.GrowingLeaders.com

Table of Contents

This small book was created to enable you—an ordinary person—to begin impacting next generation leaders in your organization. The ideas are built on the assumption that organic goals not programmatic goals are what will make the difference. Instead of merely hunting for a set number of leaders to fill existing, vacant positions, we suggest you nurture an environment where everyone catches the "virus" of servant-leadership. Start small. Stay focused. Don't quit. John Wesley changed the spiritual landscape of England in the 18th century with only 1½ to 2% of the British population on board with his Methodist movement. Martin Luther King Jr. transformed civil rights in the U.S. in the 1960s with only 1% of the American population involved. Both were sub-cultures that changed the national culture. To this end, we dedicate this book to all the churches, campuses and organizations who will act as gardeners and cultivate the soil of their team in order to grow transformational leaders. May your tribe increase.

Dr. Tim Elmore

Dr. Art Fuller

WWW.GROWINGLEADERS.COM

Chapter One
What is a Leadership Culture?

Tom Jacobs raced up the big stone slab steps glancing at his watch. He was running later than he planned. He had scheduled a 1:30 p.m. appointment with University President Dave Anderson and it was now 1:28 p.m. "If I had just started 15 minutes earlier, I'd already be seated outside his office," he thought to himself. But, then metro traffic was unpredictable. You might start early and arrive late anyway, or, start late and arrive close to on time. Go figure. He dashed out of the elevator and down the marble-floored hallway and into President Anderson's office.

"Hello, Mrs. Colson. How are things going for you today?" "Just fine, Tom. It's good to see you again. It's been awhile, hasn't it?" "Yes, it has," Tom replied collecting himself and straightening his tie. "I'll let President Anderson know you are here," said Mrs. Colson. "Fine. Thanks."

Joyce Colson was right. It had been some time since Tom had been at the University. He had graduated some twenty years earlier and went off to a successful career in business. President Anderson had been the Dean of Students back then and Tom had gotten to know him quite well. He always seemed to have a wise perspective on various issues and had given Tom good advice on more than one occasion. They had kept in touch via email and an occasional call but now Tom really wanted his insight. He was facing one of the biggest challenges of his new, albeit, recent career.

Dave Anderson walked out into the foyer of his office and greeted Tom with a hug. "Tom, it's great to see you again. How are Beverly and the boys doing? Do you want something to drink while we talk?" Tom waved off the drink but replied that his wife and sons were doing well. "Actually, President Anderson, you might remember that my boys are in high school now. Matt is a senior and Andrew is a freshman. I guess pretty soon, Bev and I will have to come to grips with 'empty-nest syndrome.'"

"Tom, first of all it's Dave, not President Anderson. And secondly, once you get an extended taste of 'empty-nest-syndrome,' I think you guys will quickly adjust to the freedom, believe me."

They strode into Dave's wood-bedecked office and parked themselves on the couch and chair over in the corner by the balcony window overlooking the campus.

"Tom, it's really good to see you again. But, I know you came to see me for a reason. What can I do to help you? You mentioned something the other day about a career change. What's up?"

"That's right," Tom responded, a little waver in his voice. "As you know, I left the University and went to work in the Marketing Department of a Fortune 500 company." Tom was searching for the right words to convey his point. "Dave, I made good money, got to travel, and met a lot of interesting people. But, after twenty years, something began to gnaw at me on the inside. I felt that while I was making a good living for my family, and was active in my church and community doing occasional volunteer work, something was missing. There just wasn't the sense of significance that I wanted from my job." Dave Anderson seemed to be listening intently.

"I really felt that I wanted to change careers and do something with the second half of my life that was based on significance and leaving a legacy instead of simply earning a paycheck." Tom's voice trailed off as he wondered what Dave must have been thinking. "Between my bonuses, stock options, and early retirement package, I was able to leave the company and go into something different. Something I think will give me that sense of fulfillment I have been craving."

Dave moved to the edge of his seat as he asked, "O.K., Tom. You've got my attention now. What career did you move into? Are you planning to be a missionary or something?" "Well, yes, and no, I suppose," Tom answered enjoying the quizzical look he was getting from his old friend. "Yes, I am going into a position of ministry, but no, I am not becoming a missionary; At least not in the traditional sense."

"Well, what sense are we talking about, my boy?"

Tom responded, "I guess in the sense that I am a missionary to our post-modern culture trying to help people see their need for a relationship with God. I have accepted a staff position at a large metropolitan church here in the area as their Executive Pastor."

"That's great, Tom!" replied Dave. "I couldn't be happier for you. With your administrative and business skills, you'll be a natural. Fantastic!"

> IF WE DON'T MAKE A MASSIVE EFFORT TO TRAIN AND DEVELOP LEADERS, WE'RE GOING TO SINK BEFORE WE GET TOO FAR OUT OF PORT.

"Well, you're right, Dave. My business background will be a big help to me but I've got no experience in ministry. Zero. Zippo. Zilch. That's why I came to see you."

Dave Anderson moved back in his chair and grinned. "I'd like to say you came to the right place for help. But, honestly Tom, I don't have a clue when it comes to leading a ministry. I mean I attend church regularly, and collect the offering once in awhile, you know, but…"

"Dave, you might not be a minister but you do have experience in an area where our church is facing a critical problem."

"And that area is…?" Dave quizzed.

"Leadership development," Tom shot back. "We are growing so fast in our attendance that we don't have enough leaders to keep the ship moving

> **THE PROBLEM YOU ARE FACING CAN ONLY BE SOLVED BY BUILDING A CULTURE OF LEADERSHIP.**

forward. If we don't make a massive effort to train and develop some leaders, I'm afraid we're going to sink before we get too far out of port."

As he listened, Dave reflected back on the work he had done the past six to eight years. When he became University president, he faced a similar situation. There just didn't seem to be enough leaders to go around at the school. They had numerous problems and issues that were going unaddressed all because he couldn't personally become involved in each one. He had felt a little bit like Moses leading the children of Israel out of the wilderness; especially the part where Moses had to respond to every issue, every complaint, big or small, which the people brought to him each day. He had realized not too soon that what he needed to develop was a leadership culture within the University system. An environment where people took ownership of problems, worked in a self-directed manner to solve them, and didn't care so much about who got the credit.

"Help" was the word that jolted Dave back to reality. Actually, Tom had said, "I really need your help," but Dave had just caught the last word as he snapped back into the moment.

"Tom, what you are talking about will take a massive effort on your part. You don't need to simply train a few leaders. The problem you are facing can only be solved by building a culture of leadership."

"Dave," Tom responded, "I know something about organizations, and leadership, and keeping employees happy, etc. But, what do you mean when you say 'culture of leadership?' That sounds like a ten-dollar consulting word."

"Well, Tom, we've determined we can boil it down to this simple definition: A leadership culture is an environment of shared values, systems, relationships and behaviors that contagiously affect team-members to think and act like servant-leaders. That's what we're trying to build here." He paused to think, and then added, "Tom, leadership researchers have discovered that two qualities differentiate an average organization from an exceptional one. First, they have more leaders at more levels than average organizations. Second, current leaders within exceptional

> A LEADERSHIP CULTURE
> IS AN ENVIRONMENT
> OF SHARED VALUES,
> SYSTEMS, RELATIONSHIPS
> AND BEHAVIORS THAT
> CONTAGIOUSLY AFFECT
> TEAM-MEMBERS TO
> THINK AND ACT LIKE
> SERVANT-LEADERS.

organizations develop and train up coming leaders. In fact, one researcher was quoted as arguing 'every seasoned leader should be a teacher' or mentor for emerging leaders."

"That's an interesting perspective, Dave. But, what would make people think there's a connection between culture and leadership? Isn't culture kind of like movies, and books, and plays? What does that have to do with leadership?" questioned Tom.

Dave pondered a research paper he had read recently citing the connection between leadership and culture. The author had claimed that, "Organizational cultures are created in part by leaders, and one of the most decisive functions of leadership is the creation, management, and sometimes destruction of culture."

"I definitely agree with that," Tom replied. "I've seen good cultures and bad cultures in organizations, and almost always I could trace it back to the leader."

"Precisely!" Dave shot back. "Every organization has a culture—either by default or design. And I've concluded that great leaders work on the culture more than the program. They set organic goals not just programmatic goals."

"That sounds interesting. Explain what you mean."

"Well, programmatic goals are what we've set for years. They usually involve numbers, budget and attendance. The trouble is, they frequently depend on artificial motivation. The numbers push us to act, instead of natural, organic motivation. We look to increase the budget by 20% or we try to recruit fifteen more leaders. This isn't bad, but it's synthetic. Organic goals use natural motivation. They work like a

> GREAT LEADERS WORK ON
> THE CULTURE MORE THAN
> THE PROGRAM. THEY SET
> ORGANIC GOALS NOT JUST
> PROGRAMMATIC GOALS.

gardener who cultivates the soil and enriches that garden with nutrients so that all the plants grow in a healthy manner. The environment affects them all, not just a few. Similarly, a leadership culture affects everyone, not just the positioned leaders."

'Pretty strong statement in support of the connection between the two ideas,' he thought. "Tom, let me break it down for you. Let's start with the notion of leadership. What do you think it is?"

Confidently Tom responded, "Leaders are the person or persons that can take people to the mountain! They are out in front, leading the charge, taking the bullets if they have to. Leadership, I suppose then, is the art of taking people to the mountain or taking bullets, or something like that."

"Well," Dave answered, "Kind of like that, I guess. What would you say to the idea that leadership is influence and leaders are change agents? They are supposed to be looking ahead, down the proverbial path to see what obstacles, roadblocks, or hurdles are in the way of the organization as it journeys toward implementing its vision and accomplishing its mission."

"I'd say that's pretty heavy, Dave. Do leaders do all of that—that stuff about looking down the path and implementing a vision, etc.?"

> **CULTURE IS AN ENVIRONMENT WHERE PEOPLE HAVE SHARED VALUES, BEHAVIORS AND QUALITIES THAT SET THEM APART FROM OTHERS.**

"Good leaders do," Dave answered. "When they see an impediment in the road, leaders are supposed to react with strategies, plans, and methods that enable the organization to adapt, or overcome the obstacle."

"Okay. So a good leader adapts and overcomes—kind of a Marine Corps thing. But what does that have to do with culture?" Tom queried.

"I guess a quick definition of culture is 'how we do things around here.' That's pretty simplistic but it captures the essence of the idea."

"Is that it? 'How we do things around here?'" asked Tom.

"Well. Cultural experts would say there are many more aspects to culture. Things like organizational values, beliefs, customs and traditions, group norms, shared meanings, habits of thinking, espoused values, climate, implicit rules or 'ropes,' and root metaphors or symbols that groups develop to characterize themselves...." Dave paused, realizing Tom was on information overload. "Maybe we could summarize it by saying, 'Culture is an environment where people have shared values, behaviors and qualities that set them apart from others.' That's why I defined a leadership culture the way I did earlier—an environment of shared values, systems, behaviors and experiences that contagiously affect team members to act like servant-leaders. It's all about the environment."

Tom leaned back and made a spinning top motion with his index finger. "Whoa, Dave. 'How we do things around here' is starting to sound better and better. With all of these other terms and concepts, why do we even need the word culture?"

"Because culture implies two critical elements beyond these concepts: structural stability and integration. Structural stability refers to the notion that culture deals with something deeply shared and stable—deeply shared could also mean less visible and less tangible. Integration, on the other hand, implies how or by what method something or someone is tied into the larger paradigm of the organization. Rituals, values, climate, and behaviors all help to bind an organization together into a coherent entity. Culture can help acclimate a person into a new organization by spelling out the behaviors and shared assumptions generally accepted by the group," replied Dave. "Think about a culture overseas. Take Kenya, Africa, for instance. Each morning as mothers send their children to school, they don't have to tell those kids to act like Kenyans. Why? Because they're surrounded by the Kenyan environment. They will naturally act that way."

> ORGANIZATIONS THAT DEVELOP LEADERSHIP ENVIRONMENTS ARE BEING REWARDED WITH SIGNIFICANT GAINS IN RETENTION, LOYALTY, AND EVEN GREATER IMPACT TO THE BOTTOM LINE.

"Tom, it's just like when you were here at the University. There were certain behaviors, values, and traditions that you became aware of and eventually adopted—all as a part of you becoming integrated into 'how we do things around here.'"

"Dave," interjected Tom, "I think I appreciate the value of leadership and understand the idea of culture now. But, how do these two things tie together and become a 'leadership culture?' Why should any company, church, or school be concerned about creating a 'leadership culture?'"

Dave leaned in knowing he had Tom's full attention now. "One article I just read indicates that organizations that develop leadership environments are being rewarded with significant gains in retention, loyalty, and even greater impact to the bottom line."

"Bottom line. Now, that's something I can relate to. In business, it's all about the bottom line. I can also see the benefit of keeping good employees and not having to be constantly replacing people, and operating in training mode all the time," said Tom. "This is sounding better and better. Tell me some more."

"Tom, you know that many organizations are uncomfortable discussing the idea of 'culture' instead of talking about the 'bottom line.' Yet, studies have shown organizations that convert their culture and leadership skills into knowledgeable, inspired and innovative workers will be the most successful and competitive in the future. In a leadership culture, people are encouraged and empowered to accomplish and perform by accepting the leadership opportunities they encounter on a daily basis."

Tom shot a quick peek at his watch and realized they had been talking for over 45 minutes. He was due back at the church for a meeting with the Senior Pastor to discuss some staffing issues. One of the staff members was not performing up to expectations and it looked as though they might have to let him go. "Listen, Dave, this has been very enlightening for me. Based on what I heard you say today, I'm convinced that what we need to do over at Community Church is begin building a culture of leadership. Do you think we can get together again in a week or so to discuss this idea further?"

The University was facing an accreditation audit in the next couple of days and Dave knew that his time would be very limited as he met with the auditors and answered their questions. However, he knew the challenge Tom faced and wanted to help all he could, especially since it was one he had wrestled with himself a few years back. "Tom, I have a pretty hectic schedule over the next couple of days. I will tell you what though. Get with Joyce on your way out and have her pencil in some time early next week for us to meet again and we'll get together."

"Dave, I really appreciate it. I knew I could count on you to help me figure this situation out."

"Tom, the next time we meet, we need to discuss your culture at Community Church. You need to understand what you've got to work with. It's a fact that all organizations have a culture. The sad fact is that not all cultures are healthy. Anyway, we'll talk about it next time. Take care. Tell Beverly and the boys I said hello."

"Will do," said Tom as he stopped by Joyce's workspace. "Joyce, what does President Anderson's schedule look like for next Monday morning? It's been years, but I guess I need to become a student again."

THOUGHTS AND INSIGHTS

In pondering the argument that above average organizations will have more leaders at various levels than average firms, how does your organization measure up?

What leadership definition would be most appropriate in your own organization? Is leadership about influence? Attaining goals? Motivating employees? Adapting to change?

Organizational culture expert Edgar Schein contends that culture occurs on both conscious and unconscious levels. What are some of the conscious aspects of your organizations' culture? What are the unconscious features?

Chapter Two
Evaluating Your Environment—
Landscape or Toxic Waste Dump?

Imagine you are strolling through a beautiful forested park. Fragrant flowers have been carefully planted everywhere. Walking paths are outlined with moist chips of cypress bark. It's apparent the entire landscape has been thoughtfully manicured for maximum attractiveness. Things just seem to flow together in harmony. Tall and strong trees, shrubs, exquisite grasses, and flowers all work together to present the greatest possible eye appeal. Some organizational cultures are similar to this beautiful, manicured landscape. They are healthy, functional, and productive. There's a vibrancy and life about them that just radiates excitement and enthusiasm.

As we imagine our walk taking us to another area of the park, we are startled as we lumber upon a smelly, putrid landfill. There is no beauty here. The manicured landscape has been replaced with unsightly heaps of rotting trash, refuse, and junk. Smoke rises from one corner of the waste dump as decay has set in and caused some previously useful objects to ignite. In contrast to our beautiful, manicured park this site seems to be a breeding ground for disease and illness. Sadly, some organizational cultures are more closely aligned with the toxic landfill than the manicured landscape. They are breeding grounds for problems, gossip, illness, and trouble. Vibrancy has been replaced with lethargy and enthusiasm has been supplanted by apathy.

> **Sadly, some organizational cultures are more closely aligned with the toxic landfill than the manicured landscape.**

As we consider these two metaphoric extremes and their relationship to organizational cultures, we must ask ourselves two questions:

1. What are the characteristics and marks of a healthy organizational culture?

2. What are the attributes of an unhealthy organizational culture?

Perhaps we should entertain a third question:

How can we determine which type of culture we are currently a part of?

This is obviously a question Tom will have to address as he moves from the business world into the environment of church ministry. President Anderson had been able to transform the culture at the University, which is a combination of both business and ministry. While these two cultures do have some similarities, there are numerous differences. Tom understood the business world was about 'bottom line.' Leaders, managers, and supervisors were interested in the financial impact of decisions. In the arena of church ministry, the focus was much more on people and power; in particular who had the power? In the business world, if you needed help, you hired someone. In the ministry arena, if you needed help, you tried to find someone gifted in that area and see if they would come along your side to help out. Relying on volunteers for help and support and knowing these same people could suspend or deny their financial resources was a huge cultural shift for him. "How can we plan a budget?' he had pondered to himself, "if we don't know how much money we'll have coming in each week?" Tom will have to become a student of the organizational culture he finds himself in, if he is to continue to be effective.

> TOM WILL HAVE TO BECOME A STUDENT OF THE ORGANIZATIONAL CULTURE HE FINDS HIMSELF IN, IF HE IS TO CONTINUE TO BE EFFECTIVE.

HEALTHY ORGANIZATIONAL CULTURES

Organizational communication researcher Gerald Goldhaber reports a 'supportive climate' is crucial in creating an effective organization. The following list is not all inclusive but rather foundational to having a healthy organizational culture:

1. Encourage open and honest communication

2. Present a clear and compelling vision of the future

3. Celebrate diversity of thought

4. Place high value on trust and credibility

5. Emphasis on relationships as well as productivity

6. Understand the value of personal and professional growth

7. Embrace a sense of community

Encourage Open and Honest Communication

Healthy organizational cultures foster environments of open and honest communication. Not just vertically, but laterally. Problems or issues are not ignored in hopes that they will disappear but surfaced and dealt with in a timely and realistic manner. People are operating without hidden motives or deception. Leaders in these organizations are not looking for 'yes men or women' but employees who will express their opinions and ideas respectfully and honestly. Communication researchers have known for years that two channels of

> **Communication researchers have known for years that two channels of communication exist in every organization—formal and informal.**

communication exist in every organization—formal and informal. Formal channels include company-wide memos, newsletters and publications, and personal communication from the leader to the employees. Informal channels primarily include the 'grapevine' or 'rumor mill' that exists in every firm. Effective leaders intentionally and strategically take advantage of these informal communication opportunities because they understand that information actually moves quicker along these informal lines than formal channels. In addition to communicating, healthy cultures place value on real listening as well. They offer empathy and respect to the speaker, identifying with and sharing, and accepting their feelings and values. Confrontation, if necessary, is handled constructively and positively.

A Clear and Compelling Vision of the Future

A clear and compelling vision of the organization's future allows me as an employee or follower to stay with the organization. If what you are doing is not significant, useful, or particularly productive, why would an employee or follower stay?

> **If employees determine that what they are doing has merit, they tend to invest more of themselves into their work and environment.**

Behavioral expert Abraham Maslow concluded that in the long run, people are searching for significance in their life and work. As a leader, we must create and communicate a vision that expresses the value of the organization's mission and vision if we expect people to build their lives and dreams around it. Healthy cultures understand the value and benefit of a clear and compelling vision and seek to craft it and promote it at every opportunity. Why? Because a clear and compelling vision of the future that followers can identify with promotes positive attitudes, high morale, job satisfaction, and productivity. If employees determine that what they are doing has merit, they tend to invest more of themselves into their work and environment. Pastor Andy Stanley in his relevant book *Visioneering*, claims vision weaves four things into our daily experience:

1. *Emotion* which reinforces our commitment.

2. *Motivation* which gives us staying power.

3. *Direction* which simplifies decision-making.

4. *Purpose* which gives us a reason to get up, show up, and accomplish our goal.

CELEBRATE DIVERSITY OF THOUGHT

Have you ever heard someone say, "Get a new thought"? Or perhaps you've seen the acronym MOTSH—'more of the same, harder.' I love the question: 'When was the last time you did something for the first time?' What these ideas are trying to communicate is that occasionally we need to think in new and different ways. Many times, doing more of the same, only harder will not solve our problems. Albert Einstein was reported to have said that we cannot solve a significant problem at the same level of thinking we were at when we first created it. One strategy for

> **WHEN WAS THE LAST TIME YOU DID SOMETHING FOR THE FIRST TIME?**

solving problems, suggested by creativity researcher Roger von Och in his fascinating book *A Kick in the Seat of the Pants*, was to look for the 'second right answer.' In other words, don't accept the same answers all of the time in attempting to solve problems—try thinking something different. In a healthy culture, the ability and privilege to think 'outside the box' is encouraged and supported, not ridiculed or belittled. A side benefit of appreciating diversity of thought and opinion is that is encourages open discussion and productive conflict management.

PLACE HIGH VALUE ON TRUST AND CREDIBILITY

The downsizing and restructuring of the past decade or so have led to an erosion of trust in many organizations. Employees feel that the 'psychological contract' they had with their employer has been violated and broken. In the past, employees believed that a company would provide long-term employment and reasonable benefits if they provided a fair day's work. However, in today's fluid and free-agent environment, companies are more likely to review and question every position periodically to determine its value to the corporate bottom line. For many, trust and credibility are in short supply. Yet, trust is the glue that binds the organization together according to author and leadership guru, John Maxwell. Leaders and organizations have to build on integrity, concern and results, to be successful in the future, says Robert Shaw in his work, *Trust in the Balance*. Organizational researchers, James Kouzes and Barry Posner, argue credibility and trust have to be earned and built over time. Our ability to display and demonstrate trust in other people actually helps them to trust us. Being candid about our behavior, especially when others might see it as inconsistent or incompatible with what we've done or said previously, can encourage people to trust us. In a healthy organizational culture, trust and credibility are the norm. Proven leaders have demonstrated their reliability through their past behavior and by being up-front in dealing with issues.

> **TRUST IS THE GLUE THAT BINDS THE ORGANIZATION TOGETHER.**

EMPHASIS ON RELATIONSHIPS AS WELL AS PRODUCTIVITY

Futurist and sociologist Leonard Sweet believes we are entering into the relationship economy. We've moved through the information, service, and experience economies but the capital of the future will be relationships. Why? Because as humans, relationships are critical to our mental, emotional, and spiritual well-being. None of us lives on an island (except in the TV show Survivor). The World Wide Web has demonstrated our interconnectedness through the vast networks of interlinked computers and servers that tie us together and permit the sharing of information and emails. Healthy organizational cultures understand this fact and promote relationships and cooperation. They realize if people are more related and connected, they tend to work together more to solve problems, develop ideas, and implement new and more effective strategies for achieving the organization's goals and mission.

> **WE ARE ENTERING INTO THE RELATIONSHIP ECONOMY.**

UNDERSTAND THE VALUE OF PERSONAL AND PROFESSIONAL GROWTH

Organizations with healthy cultures recognize, as employees gain additional knowledge and skills, that both the organization and employee benefit. Personal and professional development consultant Brian Tracey contends, "If you're not getting better, you're getting worse." Individuals, like companies, have to develop competencies if they are to stay fresh, viable, and marketable especially in today's free agent economy. Most people sense this. They understand and realize the need to improve their expertise to remain competitive in the workplace. The problem is sometimes

> You may wonder, "What if I equip my ineffective team members to be more effective and they decide to leave?" Consider instead: What if you don't—and they stay?

organizations do not realize this about employees. They are either unwilling or uninterested in supporting an employee's desire to gain additional skills for fear the person might leave the organization to work elsewhere. I met recently with a manager who asked: "What if I equip my ineffective team members to be more effective and they decide to leave?" I just smiled and replied: "What if you don't—and they stay?" Organizations with healthy cultures go out of their way to support, contribute, and encourage employees to gain additional proficiency understanding it will enhance job satisfaction and productivity in the long run.

Embrace a Sense of Community

Having a sense of community is important to healthy organizations. There is a realization that people crave community and belonging and want to be a part of something significant. It's in our DNA. The benefit to the organization is when 'community' truly exists, people are more productive, satisfied, and excited about their work and the organization's mission. They don't simply punch in and punch out but discuss the work, the vision, and mission with their coworkers, friends, and family. It becomes part of who they are. They are looking for new ways to accomplish the work, bouncing ideas off of each other, and questioning the process. Collaboration among team members becomes the modus operandi rather than the exception to the rule. Leadership experts James Kouzes and Barry Posner suggest people "need opportunities to socialize, exchange information, and solve problems informally." These opportunities can be accomplished more readily in an organization that touts and promotes a sense of community among its members.

Toxic Cultures

If healthy cultures are characterized by 'supportive climates,' it can be said that toxic cultures typically have 'defensive climates.' Many of us have encountered, either firsthand or vicariously through listening to the woes of friends, a toxic organizational culture. These environments are breeding grounds for problems, gossip, bad attitudes among workers, insecurity, defensive attitudes, and strife between leaders and followers. We won't spend a great deal of space elaborating here about the characteristics of unhealthy organizational cultures, but let's take a quick snapshot of such a place. Toxic cultures typically exhibit characteristics like:

1. Control and manipulative strategies: People attempt to trick others, negatively influence their attitudes, or manipulate their behavior.

2. Evaluative – There's plenty of blaming, passing judgment on others, and questioning the values and motives of others.

3. Dogmatic – People are more concerned about being right and winning than being effective and productive.

4. Superiority – People communicate an attitude of superiority in their position, status, and abilities while trying to arouse feelings of inadequacy in those around them.

5. Unconcern – The welfare of others is secondary. Employee feelings, ideas, and interests are disregarded and considered unimportant. The achievement of the 'goal' is all-important regardless of the methods or means.

6. Dishonest and confrontational – Suspicion and distrust are common. Responses and behaviors are couched in self-seeking desires, and confrontation is hostile and threatening rather than constructive.

WHAT KIND OF CULTURE DO YOU HAVE?

The all-encompassing question for each of us that are a part of any organization is, "Does this organization have a healthy or toxic culture? How can I know the difference?" One way to measure the healthiness of your organization's culture would be to do an informal cultural audit. Consider your organization in the following areas:

> **THE BENEFIT TO THE ORGANIZATION IS WHEN COMMUNITY TRULY EXISTS, PEOPLE ARE MORE PRODUCTIVE, SATISFIED, AND EXCITED ABOUT THEIR WORK AND THE ORGANIZATION'S MISSION.**

1. Communication

2. Relationships

3. Training and development

4. Values

5. Structure

And ask the following questions:

1. Does my organization place a high priority on these elements?

2. How is this priority demonstrated? Investment of time? Resources?

3. What are the stories, artifacts, and beliefs that seem important to our organization?

4. Is this some aspect of the organization's culture that is hindering fulfillment of the mission/vision?

5. How does our organization define leadership?

6. What are the basic underlying principles and assumptions by which our organization operates?

7. How is conflict handled in our organization?

8. How are influence, power, and authority distributed in our organization?

9. How are rewards and punishment allocated in our organization?

10. What level of participation is expected in our organization?

Again, while these questions are not all inclusive, they should be sufficient to get you started on deciphering whether your organization has a healthy or toxic cultural environment. If it's deemed healthy, great! You can move on toward developing a leadership paradigm there. If it's unhealthy in some area, you may want to give attention and focus to reviewing what the issues are and implementing some positive and necessary cultural changes before launching into leadership development.

In Tom's case, he will need to examine and measure the culture there at Community Church before moving very far ahead with his plans for creating a leadership culture. His next steps and effectiveness very much will depend on how well the formal and informal communication systems there are working. Depending on what has happened between the leadership and congregation in the recent past, he may have some trust or credibility issues to overcome first. He was smart enough to know that if people didn't trust you, they won't follow you very long. Tom also wanted to re-examine Community Church's Mission and Vision Statement. Was it up to date? Was it realistic and memorable? He wasn't sure but he was determined to find out.

Thoughts and Insights

What are the essential elements of a mature organizational culture?

Why do you think cultures are so resistant to change?

If you could change three things about your present organizational culture, what would they be?

CHAPTER THREE

Vision and The Principle of Creative Tension: Mind the Gap

Tom was especially thankful this morning that Starbucks opened at 6:30 a.m. He hadn't been a big coffee drinker until he had attended the University. But, once there, he quickly became aware coffee was the magic elixir that ran through everyone's veins. Students drank it to help them stay up late the night before exams. They met in the Student Union to share a cup of java and commiserate with one another about a particular class, teacher, or life in general. Thinking back, he realized how carefree those days had been. 'Isn't it a shame you don't know how good you've got it until you're through it' he mused.

He got in line right behind a guy that looked like his life depended on getting a cup of coffee. "I'll have a half-caf, sugar free, non-fat, vanilla latte with a pack and a half of sweetener," he heard the young man articulate. 'Man, this guy knows his coffee,' Tom thought as he stepped forward to order a Venti black 'coffee of the day.' He anxiously glanced around looking to see if Dave was sitting in any of the big high back chairs or at one of the tables. Dave Anderson had agreed to meet him this morning but because they both had pretty full schedules, early morning seemed like the best bet to link up. Meanwhile, the barista handed him his coffee and change. Not seeing Dave, he decided to plant himself in a cushy chair over by the window where he could keep an eye out for him.

Tom didn't have to wait long. Within a couple minutes, Dave strode in the door, Styrofoam cup in hand. Tom stood up and waved to Dave, "I'm over here. Is that a cup of coffee you've got, Dave? I was planning to buy you one this morning." Reaching out to shake Tom's hand, Dave explained, "Normally, I would let you. But, I still struggle with paying three bucks for a cup of coffee I guess. Old habits die hard. I stopped down at the Stop-n-Go station and grabbed a cup. Thanks anyway."

"Dave, let me say I really appreciate you taking time out of your schedule to meet with me, especially this early in the morning," Tom began. "Well, you're quite welcome, Tom. I want to see this thing work out for you. And besides, you really piqued my interest after our last conversation. That email about organizational culture, and how you were in the process of evaluating Community Church's environment got my attention. I knew you were serious then."

Tom leaned in as he said, "Dave, I think I understand the issues surrounding culture and how to recognize the signs of a healthy culture or an unhealthy one. At Community Church, we have some work to do, but in general, I think things are in pretty fair shape, culturally speaking."

"The thing that's grabbed my attention," he continued, "is this 'vision thing.' In business, we let our employees know what we expected of them, what our goals and quotas were, and expected them to help us get there." Dave responded, "I suppose you're finding the church world to be somewhat different. Is that it?"

> **NOTHING TRULY HAPPENS IN AN ORGANIZATION UNTIL THERE IS A VISION.**

"Different is an understatement," Tom replied. "We've got all of these volunteers we have to motivate and train. It doesn't seem you can push them too hard because they may just decide to stop helping. Pastor John says we have to spend time 'casting vision' if we are going to get them motivated and involved. I know where we want to go, but it seems like we're so far from where we need to be. What's your take on 'vision,' Dave? Is it really that important?"

Dave sat back in the oversized chair and slowly but carefully said, "Nothing truly happens in an organization until there is a vision." He allowed the words to soak in before proceeding further. "Tom, our son Aaron recently visited London, England. He came back telling us all about his trip, the people he had met, and places he had seen while in Europe. One of the most intriguing things he discovered was the London subway system, known affectionately by locals as 'the Tube.' What amused him was the pre-recorded message that the synthesized voice always spouted as the railcar doors were closing—"Mind the gap," meaning 'watch your step' as you are getting onto the train. Many times as we survey our organization, we quickly become aware of the gap between our vision and our reality."

"We've got a gap alright," sighed Tom. "When I think about the gap between our reality and where we need to go, at times I get downright depressed."

Dave said, "That's natural, Tom. Gaps can be discouraging, and even zap our enthusiasm. But on the other hand, gaps can be a great source of creative energy. Think of it this way—without a gap between the current reality and your vision, there would be little incentive to move forward with implementing the vision."

"Dave, I honestly hadn't thought of it like that," replied Tom. "Pastor John was saying the other day how vision has to be specific and how it's a picture of a desired future for our organization. In fact, he felt we could use our vision to help us measure and mark our success. I'll tell you, Dave, when we start talking about casting vision for the future and trying to generate enthusiasm in the present, sometimes it feels like a David and Goliath moment."

As Tom spoke, Dave reflected on his tenure as University president. He had known the struggle of turning an organization around and implementing change. He had spent many a meeting with faculty and staff trying to hone the Mission and Vision statements of the school. But, he wanted to go beyond just having a great sounding statement and really bring about a process of excellence in every aspect of the school's operations.

"Tom, are you familiar with the writing of Peter Senge?" Dave questioned.

"I have heard the name, Dave, but I am not sure I know much about his work," Tom answered quizzically.

"Peter Senge," Dave began, "in his book, *The Fifth Discipline*, refers to this gap we've been talking about as 'creative tension' and likens it to a rubber band being stretched. One end of the rubber band represents 'reality as we know it' in your organization today. The other end symbolizes your vision. As we stretch the rubber band it creates a tension between your reality and your vision. The tension we experience can include pressures, frustrations, occasional failures, and even anxiety. This tension seeks either release or resolution and there are only two ways for it to resolve itself—pull the vision down toward reality or pull reality up toward the vision. We want to ensure reality is pulled up toward the vision. In order to do this, we must take action."

Tom quickly responded, "I feel the stretch. No doubt about that. And, I've experienced some of the frustrations and anxieties. But, what kind of action do we take?"

"Well, one action is to adopt the attitude that your current realities will become your allies, not your enemies. Having a clear and proper understanding of the present situation is almost as important as casting a clear vision. We need to realize and accept the truth concerning our organization. If at present we don't have a leadership culture but we want to birth and grow one, accept that fact."

> HAVING A CLEAR AND PROPER UNDERSTANDING OF THE PRESENT SITUATION IS ALMOST AS IMPORTANT AS CASTING A CLEAR VISION.

Dave continued, "If there are organizational structure issues blocking your progress, admit them instead of ignoring them. If there are key people whose attitudes and behaviors are causing a problem in moving toward the vision, deal directly with them as best as you can. The Law of Problems says if you ignore a problem, it will come back to bite you. If we surface a problem and attempt to deal with it honestly, it can potentially become an opportunity. The bottom line is having a realistic view of your current circumstances."

"Okay Dave, let's say I get a good understanding of our reality, and I adopt the attitude that this situation is my ally, not my enemy. I'm convinced. But, how do I get other people in the organization to move forward and embrace the vision?" questioned Tom.

"Three things," said Dave. "Let me give you three things you can do to help move others toward your vision of an organization with a leadership culture. And, Tom, since you're in a church, I've labeled these three things with 'Es' to help you remember them better. This stuff may just preach." Dave drew a long breath before beginning, "The first one is *envisioning*. It involves setting high expectations and consistently modeling the behaviors we want others to emulate. However, it requires more than modeling. Another aspect of this process is to articulate a compelling vision that people can commit to accomplish."

> **BIG VISIONS ENGENDER SUPPORT AND EXCITEMENT. SMALL VISIONS PRODUCE APATHY AND DISINTEREST.**

Tom was scribbling quickly to make sure he got everything Dave had said. "Got it. Envisioning. What's next?"

"Next comes *enabling*," Dave intoned. "*Enabling* is accomplished through expressing personal support for team members as they try to perform in the face of challenging objectives. It means providing whatever resources and strategy they need to act. Expressing your confidence in people helps provide the psychological encouragement that is sometimes needed as they move toward the vision."

"Dave, this is good stuff. *Envisioning, Enabling*. What's next?" queried Tom.

"The third thing is *energizing* and it means demonstrating personal excitement and energy for the vision and leveraging your enthusiasm through personal contact with various groups of people in the organization. If the leader is not personally excited by the prospect of accomplishing the vision, why should he or she expect the followers to be motivated to take action?" Dave remarked.

Tom was still writing furiously as Dave stopped to sip his coffee. Dave wished now he *had* bought a Starbucks coffee. These Styrofoam cups just didn't do much for the taste he thought. Tom leaned back in his chair as he finished jotting down the last sentence. He wanted to close his eyes and rest a minute but he knew Dave's time was limited. He should better press on while he could. "I can see," he exclaimed, "that this vision thing is bigger than what I thought it was. In fact, it sounds kind of like one of the major keys to making this leadership culture idea work."

Dave responded, "It definitely is, Tom. You may not have read any of his stuff yet, but going into the ministry field, you'll encounter it soon enough—George Barna. He has written some great stuff on vision, why it's important, and how it can help your organization accomplish its goals."

"Can you give me just s synopsis of some of his ideas, Dave?" asked Tom.

"I'll do my best, Tom. But, you should definitely pick up his book on vision. Good stuff. Anyway, Barna suggests that vision benefits an organization in several ways. Among them: helping you to dream big. Many times we confine our vision to what we already know and understand. However, vision should encourage us to dream big. Think about your organization and where you want to go on a grand scale! Big visions engender support and excitement. Small visions produce apathy and disinterest. Leadership author John Maxwell has said, "No one ever raised big money for a project like painting the church restroom." If you want to elicit enthusiasm and commitment, dream big. Someone has said, "It's easier to raise a million dollars for a cathedral than $500 for a dishwasher."

'Here we go again,' Tom thought silently. He leaned forward, clutched his pen and began to write. He wrote, 'Dream Big' in bold letters and underlined the phrase.

"Tom, the second thing vision does is provide a sense of continuity to your organization; A common thread or theme that runs from the past into the future. Many times organizations, especially churches and schools, frequently change plans and goals as new leaders come and go. A long-term vision helps build a bridge from today into the future without ignoring your past," said Dave.

'Continuity,' Tom wrote down. "That makes sense. I've seen numerous situations where an organization did a 180-degree about face in goals when a new leader came on board. It makes you wonder if anybody in charge really knows what's going on; kind of a Mission of the Month thing."

"Tom, let me know when you are getting overloaded here. You know I used to teach a lot and I'm just getting wound up. I don't want you to glaze over on me," spoke Dave.

"I'm good to go, Dave. Let it roll," said Tom.

"Okay, if you insist," Dave started. "Third, vision helps to provide direction and purpose for the organization and also for organizational members. Every decision can be measured and held up against the bright light of the vision. If it fits with the vision, it's a go. If not, we reject it for a better alternative in the future."

> **Someone has said, "It's easier to raise a million dollars for a cathedral than $500 for a dishwasher."**

'Direction and purpose,' scrawled Tom quickly, 'for the organization as well as the members.' "Okay, I got it. Anything else about vision?"

"Yes, just a couple more. Vision makes change easier to accept and vision promotes loyalty," replied Dave sitting back and swilling down some more java.

> **VISION MAKES CHANGE EASIER TO ACCEPT.**

Tom asked, "Okay, I appreciate the abbreviated version but give me just a little meat here. How does a vision make change easier?"

"Well, vision is the opposite of the status quo," said Dave. "It demands new approaches and new outcomes as we seek to implement it. When leaders explain in detail their vision for the organization, it helps to ease any sense of discomfort or uncertainty about the future. In short Tom, vision makes change more palatable for followers."

"That makes sense. If I understand what it is we're aiming at, I may be more accepting of it," replied Tom. "What about the loyalty aspect of vision though?"

"Tom, a focused vision promotes loyalty as people feel more a part of the organization by understanding its vision for change. When vision is present, we tend to shift our thinking from failure to success. As followers and employees take ownership of the vision, they are brought together in sharing the common vision. We begin to see diversity and differences as strengths rather than weaknesses," answered Dave.

"This is really some great stuff, Dave. I can't wait to get back and share it with Pastor John and some of the others on staff at Community Church," Tom said.

Dave answered, "Tom, you're right, this is good stuff. But, it's all worthless unless you do one thing." He went silent, anxious to see how Tom would react.

"Don't stop now, Dave. What one thing? I need to know," Tom replied nervously trying to fill the silent void.

Dave sat back, looked out the window and answered, "Communication."

Tom prodded him to explain. "Dave, what do you mean by communication? I mean, that's a pretty broad field."

"Vision will accomplish nothing... unless it is communicated clearly and properly. Vision has the power to do all of the

> **A FOCUSED VISION PROMOTES LOYALTY AS PEOPLE FEEL MORE A PART OF THE ORGANIZATION BY UNDERSTANDING ITS VISION FOR CHANGE.**

aforementioned positive things. It can help change your current reality into a bright future if communicated correctly," answered Dave.

"Well, how, when and where can I communicate the vision clearly and properly?" Tom questioned.

"If I were considering the communication of an organizational vision," began Dave, "I would use every channel, formal and informal, available. State the vision in your church newsletter or bulletin. Speak with small groups and one-on-ones where appropriate to discuss the vision with them. Be sure to meet with your ministry leaders from time to time to share the vision personally with them. Vary the format of your communication as much as possible to maintain a high level of interest."

"For example, do you think I could use an interview with one of our leaders in front of the church?" Tom asked excitedly.

"Tom, I would use that, and I might even use a video clip when talking about the importance of the vision. Be strategic in communicating the vision to all of the groups within your church and couch the vision in terms of benefits that each group can relate to and grasp," Dave replied. He continued, "Your goal in constantly communicating the vision, to your church, school or any organization, is to make 'vision carriers' out of others. In order to do this, the vision will have to be communicated in a clear, crisp, and compelling way. Remember Tom, clarity is in the eyes of the listener. Just because I may think I am communicating it clearly does not mean I actually am. Keep in mind the listener, their needs and questions, as you communicate. Crisp means easily repeatable. A crisp vision is one I can state succinctly from memory and explain to others. Finally, compelling means I am agreeing to go there with you. The vision is of interest and importance to me to the extent that I want to take the journey with you as the leader."

> **VARY THE FORMAT OF YOUR COMMUNICATION AS MUCH AS POSSIBLE TO MAINTAIN A HIGH LEVEL OF INTEREST.**

Dave began to notice it slowly but it was growing with each passing minute. Tom was beginning to glaze over. Dave had done a core dump on the subject of vision and Tom was struggling to take it all in. "Tom, I know that I have backed up the truck and dumped it on you today. Let's stop for now and give you some time to digest some of what we've been discussing today."

Tom lowered his pen and pad. "I agree with you. This has been good but my head is beginning to hurt. I never realized the impact and importance of vision to an organization before today."

Both men stood to their feet, clutched their coffee cups and moved toward the doorway. "The next time we get together Dave, I want to bring along Pastor John if you don't mind. He needs to hear some of this stuff," Tom said.

"Not a problem, Tom. I'd love to meet and discuss leadership with him. I imagine he can teach me a thing or two about it," replied Dave. With that they parted and each hurried off to their respective duties. Tom felt like he had already put in a day's work but was anxious to get over to the Church and talk with Pastor John about some of what he had heard today. Pastor was the kind of guy that loved to talk about leadership and leaders. Tom knew he would eat this stuff up.

Thoughts and Insights

What is your organization's vision for the future? Is it clear, crisp, and compelling?

How does your organization communicate its vision?

What's the single biggest obstacle to implementing your organization's vision?

CHAPTER FOUR
How to Bring About Cultural Change

When Tom got back to the church, he and Pastor John tossed around some ideas on their ministry vision. They prayerfully discussed how they as leaders could bring about the changes they felt God desired for their ministry. Perhaps you have sized up your organization and believe that for you to become more successful, more productive, and mission-minded, you need to implement a leadership culture. A couple of things should be revealed up front about the transformation process. First, it won't be easy and will take time. Cultural change is not usually achieved with any rapidity. Second, it will cause pain. Anytime people are forced to modify their behaviors; pain, disappointment, and frustration potentially will be present. The question is: Is the pain worth the gain? We believe it will be and counsel you to push on beyond the organizational aches. Harvard leadership professor, John Kotter, wrote an instructional book, *Leading Change*, on how to implement a change process. His ideas serve as the basis this chapter. For additional detail, we would recommend picking up a copy of his work. Kotter argues there are eight stages to the change process:

1. Establishing a sense of urgency
2. Creating a guiding coalition
3. Developing the vision and strategy
4. Communicating the change vision
5. Empowering broad based action
6. Generating short-term wins
7. Consolidating gains and producing more change
8. Anchoring new approaches in the culture

His caution in attempting change using this stage process is that many times people will be tempted, because of 'pressure to show results,' to skip various stages or move them out of sequence. Kotter counsels this almost always leads to further problems. Transforming your organization into a leadership culture will require creativity, sacrifice, and dedication to the process. If the effort is under led or over managed you run the risk of the process getting out of control or worse, floundering and dying before it reaches infancy. Let's look briefly at each of these stages of the change process.

ESTABLISHING A SENSE OF URGENCY

Without a sense of urgency, many people will not give that extra effort needed to make changes. They will resist change initiatives and cling to the status quo. Needed sacrifices will go un-made. Urgency should not be confused with anxiety. Creating anxiety will only increase resistance to the change process. Increasing urgency demands you remove or minimize any sources or impact of complacency. It may mean eliminating signs of organizational excess. It may require setting higher targets for the organization both internally and externally. Creating a sense of urgency may require changing internal measurements that focus on the wrong indices or systems. Urgency may demand more honest discussions regarding the organization's problems. Producing organizational urgency may mean taking bold and possibly risky actions; the kind we typically associate with good leadership. If caution is the prevailing wind, urgency cannot set sail, and transformation might as well be cast overboard. In the end, creating a sense of urgency may require creating a controlled crisis. Kotter claims, "Conducting business as usual is very difficult if the building is on fire."

> **WITHOUT A SENSE OF URGENCY, MANY PEOPLE WILL NOT GIVE THAT EXTRA EFFORT NEEDED TO MAKE CHANGES.**

CREATING A GUIDING COALITION

Many times the media will associate business comebacks and transformations with one larger-than-life individual—the Lee Iacoccas, Jack Welchs or Sam Waltons of the world. The truth is, transformation is rarely, if ever, the work of one individual. It takes a guiding coalition to sustain and drive the change process. There are four key elements essential to building an effective guiding change coalition:

1. Positional power – Are the key players on board? Has anyone been left out who could potentially block the progress of the group?

2. Credibility – Are coalition members taken seriously by others in the organization? Do they have reputations for integrity and honesty?

3. Expertise – Do the team members have the experience, knowledge, and discipline required to make informed and intelligent decisions?

4. Leadership – Are the group members proven leaders able to direct the change process?

Two additional elements are critical to create the team necessary to sustain the process—trust and a common goal. Without trust, it will be difficult to create

> **THE TRUTH IS, TRANSFORMATION IS RARELY, IF EVER, THE WORK OF ONE INDIVIDUAL.**

a sense of teamwork. A common goal helps to bind team members together. These two elements work in tandem.

DEVELOPING THE VISION AND STRATEGY

Successful transformations are based on vision, not decree or micromanagement. Vision presents us with a picture of a preferred future and implies why we should make every effort to help create it. Kotter claims vision does three things for the organizational change process:

1. Simplifies hundreds of detailed decisions – Question each decision in light of the vision. Does this line up with the vision?

> **A GOOD VISION IS:**
>
> **IMAGINABLE,**
>
> **DESIRABLE,**
>
> **FEASIBLE, FOCUSED,**
>
> **FLEXIBLE, AND**
>
> **COMMUNICABLE.**

2. Motivates people to take action in the right direction – Change involves pain. A good vision acknowledges that sacrifices will be necessary but also explains how these will bring about superior benefits.

3. Helps coordinate the actions of people quickly and efficiently – Vision will help align and empower people rather than require constant checking with the boss.

A good vision is: imaginable, desirable, feasible, focused, flexible, and communicable.

COMMUNICATING THE CHANGE VISION

The power of vision is only unleashed when people understand it and grasp it. Failure to communicate vision properly and sufficiently will doom your change effort, or worse, send inconsistent and inappropriate messages to those in the organization. Realizing and accepting a vision of a preferred future generates numerous questions in the minds of employees and followers. Vision communication will be best served when it is simple, direct, jargon-free, and repeated. If possible use metaphors and analogies to paint a verbal picture of the vision. Vision also needs to be communicated in many different formats—group meetings, memos, organizational newsletters, and informal one-on-one discussions. Most ideas only sink in after frequent repetition. Lastly, explain any apparent inconsistencies in the vision and be sure leaders behave in a manner consistent with the vision. Inconsistent behavior will only undermine the communication of the vision. Try to practice three items with your vision:

> **USE METAPHORS AND ANALOGIES TO PAINT A VERBAL PICTURE OF THE VISION.**

1. See it Clearly
2. Show it Creatively
3. Say it Constantly

EMPOWERING BROAD BASED ACTION

Internal transformation only occurs if people get involved in assisting the process. They won't help if they feel powerless to impact the process. Kotter explains there are four organizational obstacles that need to be attacked if we are to empower people to act. These are:

1. Structures – Inappropriate structures can fragment resources and responsibilities.
2. Skills – We are asking people to change years of habits and behaviors with minimal training and education.
3. Systems – Many times we blame lack of progress on the human tendency to resist change when the fault actually lies with bureaucratic systems that impede progress.
4. Supervisors – Supervisors who are either unwilling or incapable of implementing the vision for change can block or disrupt the process.

Identifying and confronting these obstacles can increase the chances of the change process gaining the momentum needed to reach the finish line.

GENERATING SHORT-TERM WINS

> **SHORT TERM WINS HELP PROVIDE EVIDENCE THE SACRIFICES ARE WORTH IT.**

Cynics, critics, and nonbelievers will demand to see proof of the validity of the change process. People want to see either data or results indicating the change process is actually working and not endangering the organization. Pastors trying to implement changes within their congregation in hopes of increasing the size, finances, or ministries of the church, need to produce some short-term wins to give credibility to the process. Visionary school administrators caught up in the big dream of what 'might be' must manage today's reality and get a few wins under their belt if they want to continue to be taken seriously by their academic colleagues. Short term wins help provide evidence the sacrifices are worth it. They help fine tune the vision by providing concrete data. They help to build momentum, morale, and motivation by enlisting previously neutral supporters. Lastly, they help to keep the leadership on board. Short-term wins provide evidence that the change process is on track and working properly. Note: short-term wins are not gimmicks, smoke and mirrors, or contrived results but honest improvements.

CONSOLIDATING GAINS AND PRODUCING MORE CHANGE

Kotter's one cardinal rule of change suggests: When you let up before the job is done, critical momentum can be lost, and regression may follow. Resistance to change never fully dissipates. Change opponents may be driven underground, but await an opportunity to come back and reassert themselves. Organizations are

> **WHEN YOU LET UP BEFORE THE JOB IS DONE, CRITICAL MOMENTUM CAN BE LOST, AND REGRESSION MAY FOLLOW.**

interdependent networks. As a result, changing one element impacts potentially dozens of others. All of these interdependencies can complicate change. Maintain a sense of the overall change direction and then begin to implement it one project at a time. All organizations have unnecessary interdependencies brought about by some past problem rather than current reality. Identify and eliminate as many of these as possible. Doing this may lengthen the change process but ultimately make it easier in the long run. In a successful change effort, stage seven will produce more change, not less. The credibility gained by accomplishing short-term wins will enable the guiding coalition to take on bigger projects. Additional people should be brought in and developed to help with the change process.

ANCHORING NEW APPROACHES IN THE CULTURE

If new approaches are not anchored in the organizational culture, regression will begin to take place. Slowly at first, but eventually picking up speed until all of the transformational gains will either disappear or be eroded. An organization's underlying culture will reassert its influence unless the new practices truly replace the old ones. How do we anchor new approaches in the culture? Realize that cultural change comes last, not first. Understand that new procedures, norms, and behaviors only take root as it becomes very clear they work. Appreciate the fact that sometimes the only way to change the culture is to change some of the key people. Lastly, make succession decisions based on the new culture. If leadership promotions are not compatible with the new paradigm, the old cultural will reassert itself.

> **AN ORGANIZATION'S UNDERLYING CULTURE WILL REASSERT ITS INFLUENCE UNLESS THE NEW PRACTICES TRULY REPLACE THE OLD ONES.**

THE LEADERSHIP DEVELOPMENT CYCLE

After surveying hundreds of university campuses and other organizations that develop leaders well, we've concluded that a "cycle" may be the best way to diagram how leaders are consistently developed. This cycle begins in the middle with an assessment of your present culture, then moves toward action steps which generate opportunities for people to jump into the development cycle. Note the following elements:

Organizations that develop leaders move from an assessment, to an appropriate catalytic event, where members are challenged to become students of leadership. This may be a retreat or conference sponsored by your organization. Afterward, those who respond will need follow-up resources to keep growing. Many events never become an ongoing "process" because no one provides the resources to sustain the interest and enable folks to build the principles into their lives. Next, mentoring communities can be formed to discuss and apply the principles. After that, ongoing training should occur to address the gaps that exist in the culture. Finally, leadership opportunities and apprenticeships should be established for those who are ready to play a leadership role in the organization. (There's nothing more frustrating than to be equipped for a task and then never allowed to actually do it.)

In this final stage of the cycle, potential leaders are given a chance to try out their leadership, and to be mentored as an apprentice by a present leader. This is where organizations begin to experience the power of multiplication. It involves labor—hard labor—but it is worth it. D. L. Moody once said, "It is better to train a hundred men than to do the work of a hundred men…but it is harder." Multiplication, not mere addition, is the only way to develop enough leaders for the needs of tomorrow.

> NOTHING'S MORE FRUSTRATING THAN BEING EQUIPPED FOR A TASK AND NEVER ALLOWED TO ACTUALLY DO IT.

Thoughts and Insights

In considering Kotter's plan for organizational change, where is your organization on the change continuum? Do you need to create a sense of urgency first? Does urgency exist, but there is no guiding coalition to direct it?

Essentially, change sticks only when it becomes "the way we do things around here." How would you go about demonstrating to others in your organization that specific behaviors can lead to improved organizational performance?

CHAPTER FIVE

Creating An Environment That Creates Leaders

Pastor John was climbing out of the car as Tom shut it off. They had been forced to park some distance from the auditorium because of the crowd. "Tom, I am really looking forward to this leadership conference today. I just know it will help us better understand how we can create a leadership culture at Community Church," Pastor John exclaimed eagerly.

"Joe Wellton is supposed to be one of the best when it comes to the subject, John. He pastored several churches, has started and led a few businesses and has developed numerous leaders along the way," Tom replied. "When we got the flier in the mail, I knew you would be interested. Man, look at this crowd."

They walked hurriedly up the steps, through the doors and into the expansive auditorium first stopping by the registration table to collect their notebooks. Being seated, Tom glanced at his watch noting the conference should start in five minutes. Pastor was thumbing through his notebook and registration packet. Within minutes the announcer stepped out onto the platform and introduced 'Joe Wellton.' The crowd stood to their feet clapping enthusiastically as Joe acknowledged their appreciative applause. "Thank you so much. Please be seated. We've got a lot to cover today so let's jump right in," he said.

"What church or campus ministry wouldn't want a 'leadership culture' to emerge in their midst, where leaders naturally grow and develop?" Joe started out. "The fact is most churches and schools suffer from a chronic lack of quality leaders. Staff members often have little training in leadership. They hope that lay leaders or student leaders will transfer from other places, or that they'll learn leadership simply from facing the challenges of life. Unfortunately, it usually doesn't happen that way. Often, schools and churches either have a hard time finding enough people to lead the various ministries available, or they have ill-equipped people who volunteer… or both." Tom and Pastor John were riveted to their seats. This guy was hitting the nail square on the head for them.

Joe continued, "A leadership culture emerges when someone champions the cause of leadership and works a plan to create that environment."

The house lights were lowered as a huge audio-visual projection screen was being lowered from the ceiling. The words 'Cultures arise out of movements not programs' flashed on the screen. Joe paused to let everyone read the statement and then he explained, "Programs usually start big, with a big bang, then eventually dwindle. On the other hand, movements usually start small and slowly grow very large." Joe Wellton got everyone's attention when he said, "If you study how movements began in history you'll find there is a pattern that's common for almost every one of them. A movement begins with a central man or woman. Nothing gets off the ground without a 'champion' who persistently waves the flag for the cause. The question for each of you as you consider your organization is, who should this be? Maybe the answer is 'you.'"

> A LEADERSHIP CULTURE EMERGES WHEN SOMEONE CHAMPIONS THE CAUSE OF LEADERSHIP AND WORKS A PLAN TO CREATE THAT ENVIRONMENT.

Opening his notebook, Tom wrote down the words 'Central man.' Meanwhile, Joe continued, "A movement moves from a central man to a compelling mission. The individual has to summarize the vision into a simple compelling vision for others to see and embrace. Obviously, in our discussion of a leadership culture this means someone will have to boil down this grand idea of leadership development into a simple sentence that anyone can remember. The question is: What will be your compelling mission as it relates to growing leaders?"

"Next, movements almost always involve a creative model. In other words, the central man or woman is able to point backward to a real life example of how the vision occurred in the past—and argue that it surely can happen again. Question: where's your model?"

"Next, comes a catalytic meeting. A catalytic meeting is an event where a larger number of people gather and adopt the idea. All movements experience a meeting where the values are shared and people embrace them. Your question at this point is, 'when should this be?' Are there other like-minded persons that would be interested and see the value of getting together to discuss the idea?" Tom scribbled 'Catalytic meeting' and put a question mark beside it. He thought to himself, 'It's apparent Joe Wellton used to be a pastor. Everything starts with the letter 'C' just as if he were preaching a sermon.'

"The third phase is 'Critical mass.' While everyone who comes to the catalytic event may not get involved, eventually a large enough percentage of people buy in to the idea that they impact the rest of the population. The idea gets noticed. The question is, 'Who could be a part of this? What larger group of people might this attract?'" Joe explained. "Next, we need to examine 'Community materials.' What are our transferable tools? The principles and values should be put in print, so they'll become transferable concepts. Lastly, given some time, a culture is formed that becomes a Contagious movement," Joe concluded. By this time, a diagram of these stages of the sequence were projected on the screen:

Central Man	Compelling Mission	Creative Model	Catalytic Meeting	Critical Mass	Community Materials	Contagious Movement

Pastor John leaned over and whispered to Tom, "I can see exactly what Joe is talking about here. Think about the Methodist Church. It started with a central man—John Wesley. The catalytic meetings were the circuit meetings he held. Critical mass was reached when he had 1–2 percent of the English population participating in his meetings. He was able to transform the spiritual landscape of England in the 18th century with just a fraction of the population. The tools he developed were the class meeting materials and obviously the movement that resulted was the Methodist Church. Hmmm. It makes sense to me."

The speaker announced a 15-minute break in the session and people began filing out toward the resource tables filled with books, tapes, and videos Joe Wellton had produced. Tom and Pastor John likewise visited the displays, perusing the numerous books. Tom purchased one entitled, *Mentoring Communities That Develop Leaders*. "Pastor," Tom hinted, "I'd like to go get this signed if you don't mind. I'll plan on seeing you back at our seats."

"No problem, Tom. I'm headed off to make a quick pit-stop and then I'll be right back in there."

Tom hurried back into the auditorium where Joe Wellton was busily autographing books down front. He jumped in line and waited steadily edging closer to the platform. As he reached the speaker, Tom asked, "Joe, I'm Tom Jacobs. Could you sign this, 'To Pastor John'? He doesn't know it, but I'd like to give it to him as a gift."

Joe responded, "That's great. Did you guys travel far to get here?"

"Nah, only about 30 minutes. We have been looking forward to this conference. I feel like I've already gotten several gems that were worth the ride. I'm anxious to hear what else you have to say later on."

"Thanks, Tom. I appreciate those kind remarks. I plan to talk about the 'Power of the Process' after the break. I hope you guys enjoy the day," Joe remarked.

> **IN THE CHURCH AND IN ACADEMIA, WE'VE PLACED TOO MUCH EMPHASIS ON 'EVENTS' AND FAR TOO LITTLE EMPHASIS ON 'PROCESS.'**

Tom made his way back to his seat where Pastor John was already sitting down. "Did you get your book signed?" asked Pastor. "Yes, I did. That Joe Wellton seems like a pretty good guy," Tom answered.

As Joe Wellton stepped back up on the platform he boomed, "In the Church and in Academia, we've placed too much emphasis on 'events' and far too little emphasis on 'process.' Both are necessary but we often neglect the power of the 'process.' Let me illustrate the differences for you." He began to write on an overhead projection device that had been setup during the break. "Events encourage decisions while the process encourages development." Eventually, the overhead looked like this:

EVENT	PROCESS
1. Encourages decisions	1. Encourages development
2. Motivates people	2. Matures people
3. Is a calendar issue	3. Is a consistency issue
4. Usually is about a big group	4. Usually is about a small group
5. Challenges people	5. Changes people
6. Becomes a catalyst	6. Becomes a culture
7. Is easy	7. Is difficult

"Wow," said Tom to Pastor John. "I didn't realize there was so much difference between the two. I can see why we need to have both parts of the equation though. The event is a one-time fire-them-up situation while the process actually helps people develop their leadership skills over time."

Joe grabbed their attention again when he stated, "A leadership culture will depend on the creation and wise use of two things: significant events and safe environments. Significant events are like the one you're attending today, where you are challenged to grow and stretch. Safe environments are places for transparent discussion and discovery of truth. They encourage people to grow beyond the event and participate in new levels of relationships." As he heard this, Pastor John thought to himself, 'Our role is to create the environment and God's role is to create the life change for people.'

"Obviously, the environment we create has to be relevant to lay leaders and students. Relevant environments should accomplish three things: Build bridges, turn on lights, and create thirst," Joe spoke. "Relevant environments make it possible for people to arrive at a new destination (build bridges). Relevant environments provide people with transferable truth (turn on lights). And, relevant environments motivate people to take the next step (create a thirst)."

"In this last hour," Joe started, "I want to suggest a seven step process you can use to build leaders in your church or school. It's sort of an 'accelerated leader development plan.' Here are the basic ingredients:

1. **Criteria** – You should first decide what you believe a leader should look like. What are the core qualities you want to foster in your potential leaders? Next, create a screen for selecting candidates with good leadership potential. While you may invite everybody to an event, you should strongly encourage those who are most ready. Remember, Jesus selected his disciples.

2. **Catalyst** – Plan an event that will sufficiently cast a vision for servant leadership. It may be a single evening or a weekend event, but it must be compelling, biblical, and simple. Be sure to include a vehicle for lay leaders and students to respond at the end, regarding their interest in leadership.

3. **Communities** – Following the catalytic event, allow interested attendees to "sign up" for a mentoring community where they can continue to discuss and apply the principles that were brought up at the event. Be sure the groups are small—no more than seven people in any group. These communities will help the leadership growth process take place.

4. **Challenge** – Come up with a significant challenge or problem that should be addressed in these communities. Each group could be assigned one problem to solve over six months. You might choose a group of challenges or issues that form the context of your process, i.e., problems to be solved. It's best if they are real issues, not hypothetical.

> **A LEADERSHIP CULTURE WILL DEPEND ON THE CREATION AND WISE USE OF TWO THINGS: SIGNIFICANT EVENTS AND SAFE ENVIRONMENTS.**

5. **Coaches** – These are people who will assist and facilitate the learning. At first, these could be staff members, but later you might add lay leaders or students who have experienced the process. Your coaches are key to the experience and will grow in their leadership skills along the way. They don't have to be experts, just facilitators.

6. **Consultants** – Allow your leaders in training to have exposure to internal and external experts in a variety of subject matters. These are quality leaders in the ministry, on campus, or in the community who aren't required to give lots of time, but can visit a group to offer wise counsel as needed for the emerging leaders.

7. **Curriculum** – Provide a tool or resource that enables emerging leaders to discuss and draw good conclusions about leadership along the way. Often, a bad experience can lead to a bad conclusion, and a failure to see a principle at work. This resource should equip and foster interaction.

8. **Champion** – This person is the orchestrator of the leader development process. If you are able to create a leadership culture, someone must be the champion to wave the flag and cast vision each year. Eventually, it must be a staff person if the culture is to remain."

"Folks, let me say it has been a real pleasure and joy to be with you today. I hope this material has been helpful to you and will motivate you to go back to your organization and begin developing a leadership culture!" With that, Joe Wellton stepped off the platform and the conference was over.

Pastor John and Tom slowly stood to their feet applauding. They were excited about what they had heard and would discuss it on the ride back to the church. As they stepped into the car, Tom handed Pastor the book and said, "Here, this is for you." Pastor John replied, "I thought you bought that for yourself, Tom."

"No, Pastor, I got it for you. I'll take a look at it after you've read it. Enjoy it," smiled Tom. "I'll be busy for a while, just implementing what we heard today."

Thoughts and Insights

Consider the idea, "Cultures arise out of movements, not programs." Movements begin with a central man or woman, then move to a catalytic meeting, attain critical mass, develop community materials, and finally become a contagious movement. For example:

| Central Man | Compelling Mission | Creative Model | Catalytic Meeting | Critical Mass | Community Materials | Contagious Movement |

Evaluate the statement, 'Becoming a leader is a process, not jut an event.' What role does the event play in leadership development? What role does the process play?

Author Malcolm Gladwell (*The Tipping Point*), contends that ideas, messages, and behaviors are contagious and spread like viruses do. How might you use this notion in creating a leadership culture within your organization?

CHAPTER SIX

Barriers to Creating a Leadership Culture

Barry Phegan in his insightful booklet, *Developing Your Company Culture* says "cultures develop by evolving from lower to higher levels and leadership is about helping evolution." Cultural evolution is not always a smooth process for organizations. Sometimes we run into roadblocks that prevent us from moving the organizational forward. The job of leadership is to remove the roadblocks and allow the evolution and development to continue. What kind of road blocks stand in the way of developing a leadership culture within your church or school? Several, potentially, and these might include conflict, structural issues, personnel factors, goal erosion, and communication and trust concerns. Let's take a look at how each of these could stall your progress.

CONFLICT

Organizational environment is essentially about how people relate, communicate, and resolve disputes as they go about trying to implement the vision and mission. In the eyes of many, conflict looks like a bad thing. People view it as something negative and tend to think of it in terms of a win-lose result. Author Ken Sande claims that people respond to conflict in one of three ways: They try to escape from it, they try to attack the person with whom they are in conflict, or they attempt reconciliation with the other person. In short, we can fight it, flee it, or face it.

However, several researchers have found that conflict within an organization can have many positive benefits if it is dealt with openly, discussed honestly and cooperatively. Tillet in *Resolving Conflict*, suggests conflict can "promote new ideas, encourage better understanding, strengthen personal relationships, stimulate individual growth, and facilitate more effective solutions to problems." (It kind of makes you want to go and start a conflict just to see the positive benefits, doesn't it?). In fact, organizations where conflict is discussed openly and cooperatively can find solutions that reduce costs and increase efficiency.

How should we manage conflict so we can get about the business of producing organizational and cultural change? First, change how you and your church or school view conflict. We need to avoid the mindset that conflict is a one shot situation, and begin seeing it as an ongoing opportunity for the organization to improve and learn. Second, focus on negotiation and mediation because these permit people to have the most control and power in determining their own solution. It is critical you continue to remind yourself to be redemptive. Often you can redeem both relationships and the results you're after. You'll be surprised how often you can reach a win/win solution. Lastly, develop an organizational conflict management process. We have systems for managing inventory, financial decisions, information, and production. Likewise, we also need a system for dealing with conflict. Part of this system might involve:

> **IT IS CRITICAL YOU CONTINUE TO REMIND YOURSELF TO BE REDEMPTIVE.**

1. Prevention techniques

2. Mechanisms for feedback

3. Systems for coaching and mentoring

4. Support systems for difficult cases

5. Conflict management training to better understand issues

STRUCTURAL ISSUES

Organizations like schools and churches are made up of numerous stakeholders—faculty, staff, students, laity, committee heads, board members, and many others internally and externally. When we think of structural issues, we consider two categories: organizational politics and organizational hierarchy.

Organizational politics involves people that hold positions of power and influence within the organization and how they use these to control, influence and access resources in pursuit of the vision. Researcher Anthony Cobb has suggested that there are three different levels to organizational politics—individual, coalition, and

> **AWARENESS IS ONLY THE FIRST STEP IN THE PROCESS OF DEALING WITH ORGANIZATIONAL POLITICS.**

network. Leaders need to identify those individuals who hold positions of power and are able to influence important decisions. Coalitions can be identified in a similar fashion as we look for interest groups that control key resources, or have been together for a long period of time. Change can sometimes upset these factions and cause them to try and block any changes. Lastly, we need to identify powerful networks (made up of both individuals and coalitions) by studying key linkages among these groups: Who talks to whom? Who shares similar interests and values? Who shares access to key resources?

Awareness is only the first step in the process of dealing with organizational politics. While we are watching for these individuals, coalitions, and networks to use political power plays, as leaders we must be prepared ourselves to use power and politics. This political maneuvering can go from awareness of how people feel about an issue or situation to facilitation and interaction with those who may be helping or hindering the change process. It may also require us to align and collaborate with powerful others to help achieve the desired changes. In summary, realize that power and politics are factors to be considered when you want to initiate organizational change.

Organizational hierarchy involves how the school or church is actually set up to function. Is it pyramidal with all decisions and direction coming from the top to those below? Or is it flat and horizontal allowing free and unrestricted access between all organization members? Is the organization a bureaucracy where various formal policies and procedures have been put in place, some of which can be stifling and counter productive? How your school or church is physically structured can play a major role in aiding or hindering your attempts at creating a culture of leadership. Numerous levels of bureaucracy and miles of red tape can delay implementation of new ideas and changes, and slow down your progress to a snail's pace. Eventually people will lose enthusiasm for the change process as they try to wade through all of the organizational structure. Bottom line— organize in a way that permits maximum flexibility and freedom of movement for ideas. Encourage the development of cross-functional teams to look at problems and issues. Allow departments to cooperate and collaborate on problem solving situations.

> **ORGANIZE IN A WAY THAT PERMITS MAXIMUM FLEXIBILITY AND FREEDOM OF MOVEMENT FOR IDEAS.**

PERSONNEL FACTORS

You've heard it said before, 'people are your greatest asset'. Here in the 21st century organizations are coming to recognize this fact more and more as they attempt to hire and retain the best talent. However, while people are your greatest asset and can impact your organization positively, one person or persons in the wrong place can damage your organization sometimes irreparably. We should endeavor to place people in the area where they can most effectively use their gifts and skills to positively impact the organization. No organization can achieve and sustain long-term success except through people well suited for their jobs. Matching people's giftedness to the demands of their position will enhance employee satisfaction and productivity.

How can you ensure you are best utilizing your people and increasing the productivity and job satisfaction of those within the organization? First, identify the giftedness of each employee or follower. We invest in new equipment, machinery, raw materials and services yet people are our only renewable resource most times. Find out what your people are good at and what they like to do. Make a list of all the people and endeavors already occurring on campus that foster a leadership culture. You may be surprised how much is already happening. You can affirm what's in place and be inclusive with your plans. Second, do not make any personnel decisions without identifying the giftedness of the candidate and attempting to match it to the work involved. This is especially true for 'new hires,' but also for any position that is critical to your vision or mission. Third, encourage people to share the knowledge of their gifts with others in the organization. As people clarify their gifts and motivations to others, it will be easier to put together work teams that are complimentary rather than competitive. Lastly, hold your leaders accountable for their personnel decisions. If ministry leaders and faculty understand that the organization is going to evaluate the effectiveness and wisdom of their personnel choices, this will impact the way in which they hire, promote, or transfer people.

Goal erosion

Goals are specific standards, proficiencies, or targets that you want to hit as an individual or as an organization. Attaining these goals usually takes planning, strategy and participation. Reaching goals may also require a certain level of intensity and commitment. If commitment to a goal declines, performance and intensity usually decline as well. Sometimes, the commitment to a goal by followers will slip or erode. This can be caused by any number of factors including lack of resources, time, or training needed to reach a goal. It can be caused by broken trust where followers sense that the leader is not being totally open and honest with them and therefore resist or drop-off in goal performance. Lack of feedback on a project or process can also lead to goal erosion. If people suspect the leader is not interested in their work or results, and never comments on it, they may begin to scale back their commitment. In the long run, lower morale and performance lead to lower productivity and less job satisfaction which, in turn, leads to a goal either being postponed or dropped all together.

To combat goal erosion, you as a leader need to express interest and appreciation for the work that your people are doing. Thank and affirm followers for their commitment to the ministry or work. Do everything possible to provide the necessary resources and training people, also, require to accomplish the goal and then stand back and let them do it.

COMMUNICATION AND TRUST ISSUES

For people to buy-in to your goals and attempts to create a culture of leadership in your church or school, they have to trust the leader(s). Trust has been described as 'the glue that holds the organization together.' Kouzes and Posner claim that the trust factor is the most important a leader has to deal with if they want to achieve and maintain credibility with followers. If people do not trust a leader, they will not voluntarily follow him or her, and will regard their actions and communication as suspect. Research has demonstrated that trusting other people encourages them to trust us. Distrusting them causes them to distrust and lose confidence in us. You can foster trust in your subordinates or followers by being predictable; nothing is as frustrating as working with or for a person that has unpredictable behavior. Next, communicate clearly with others what you expect and intend. Don't leave your statements open for alternative interpretation. Lastly, make few promises and keep all of them. Making promises that we don't intend to keep or treat lightly only causes problems. Tom and Pastor John are going to have to be aware of these potential barriers if they are going to successfully implement and develop a culture of leadership at Community Church.

THOUGHTS AND INSIGHTS

What roadblocks to successfully creating a leadership culture exist in your environment?

Have your organizational leaders attempted to remove or deal with these issues? If not, why not?

How does your organization handle conflict?

> TRUST HAS BEEN DESCRIBED AS 'THE GLUE THAT HOLDS THE ORGANIZATION TOGETHER.'

CHAPTER SEVEN
How to Engineer Your Vision

There's no doubt about it; All good leaders are driven by vision. They are not satisfied with maintaining the status quo. They long to take their organization somewhere. But just what is vision? For our purposes, we suggest the following definition for you to consider:

A CLEAR MENTAL IMAGE OF A PREFERABLE FUTURE, BASED ON THE BELIEF THAT IT NOT ONLY COULD BE DONE, BUT SHOULD BE DONE.

Vision is a picture held in your mind's eye of the way things could or should be in the days ahead. Vision connotes a visual reality, a portrait of a preferred future. The picture is internal and personal. Let's apply this to your campus or church. Imagine what things might look like if a leadership culture permeated the campus. What if the majority of staff and students aspired to learn leadership?

- How would it affect the classroom?

- How might it impact chapels and spiritual life?

- What would happen to student affairs?

- How could it enhance recruitment and admissions?

Eventually, you will have to paint this mental portrait inside others if you wish the vision to materialize in your organization. Just as you have used your imagination to create this view of the future, you will have to help others catch the same vision inside of them— so that they can share in its implementation. Note the components of a vision:

> **ALL GOOD LEADERS ARE DRIVEN BY VISION.**

1. **A clear mental image** (It serves as a sort of blueprint on the inside).

2. **A positive change** (It involves improving present conditions).

3. **A future focus** (It furnishes direction to the unseen future).

4. **A gift from God** (It is divinely inspired, not humanly manipulated).

5. **A chosen people and time** (It is for a select leader and group at a given time).

> **VISION CONNOTES A VISUAL REALITY, A PORTRAIT OF A PREFERRED FUTURE.**

THE BIRTH OF A VISION

You will notice that the conception and birth of a vision is much like the birth of a child. It's a process that isn't completed overnight. Consider this process and the following stages:

1. Intimacy

This is the place of beginnings. People who catch a vision do so because they have spent time with God, receiving from Him in quietness, solitude and reflection. This is when all the work and business make sense as you reflect on how to respond to it from His perspective.

2. Conception

At times during this reflection time, a vision is conceived. Often, God provides it, in infant form. It may still be fuzzy, without all of the details—but it is real and forming inside. Just like a baby, the vision looks a lot like both mom and dad. It looks like God in its size and scope, but it looks like you, in that it fits your gifts and passion.

3. Gestation

This period of time is often the longest stage of the process. During this time the leader identifies with the problem; intercedes for the people and intervenes in the process. This period is the time when many leaders abort the vision, thinking it's just taking too long.

4. Labor

This stage is often the most painful. Just as a woman's birth pains increase in intensity and frequency—so the fight intensifies just before the vision is fulfilled. Usually, just before a vision is fulfilled, the labor is the toughest and the temptation to quit is greatest.

> **USUALLY, JUST BEFORE A VISION IS FULFILLED, THE LABOR IS THE TOUGHEST AND THE TEMPTATION TO QUIT IS GREATEST.**

5. Birth

Finally, the vision is born. All that has been going on inside the heart of the leader is ultimately realized. Everyone can now see the fruit of the prayer, planning and work. Many people show up to celebrate with you, as if they knew all along it would work out. Your temptation will be to shun them—don't—let them celebrate the "birth" with you and invite them to walk beside you in the next vision.

While most visions share the same essential qualities, there are important differences between a man-made vision and a God-made vision. For instance:

Man-Made Vision	God-Given Vision
1. You create it based on your gifts and skills.	1. You receive it as a revelation from God
2. Its fulfillment rests on staying ahead of others	2. Its fulfillment rests on the person's obedience
3. Other similar organizations are seen as competitors	3. Other similar organizations are seen as complimentary
4. Its goal is to build your organization and revenue	4. Its goal is to serve people, advance God's rule and to honor God
5. Stress may emerge both inwardly and outwardly	5. It is accompanied by inward peace and outward opposition
6. May be dropped for something better	6. Compelling and captivating until fulfilled

Given the ministry that Pastor John and Tom are involved in, they will need to evaluate whether they are operating with a God-made vision or a man-made one.

Communicating the Vision to Others

As a vision-caster, you will want to incarnate these analogies for your people:

Three Word Pictures…

1. Artist

You are painting pictures inside of the people who hear you.

2. Prophet

You are speaking words of conviction about the future, prophetically.

3. Lobbyist

You are representing a cause, compelling people to join you in the effort.

Tools to Cast Your Vision...

More than fifty years ago, Winston Churchill was a master at communicating vision to the British people during World War II. As Prime Minister, he developed a pattern that we might call the "Sir Winston Method." The pattern includes five tools...

Tool One: Strong Beginning

Churchill knew to capture and hold people's attention, you needed a strong beginning. You must grab their attention early with a compelling statement, story, fact, or quote. This draws the listener to the vision.

Tool Two: Simple Language

Churchill always spoke in simple terms that everyone could grasp and relate to. His goal was to impact the people, not impress them. His language was simple and memorable.

Tool Three: One Theme

Churchill understood that focusing on one theme at a time was the most effective way to clearly get your message across. He drilled his point home in a variety of ways, finding vivid ways to color it and a variety of ways to repeat it.

Tool Four: Pictures

Churchill painted word pictures for his listeners to visualize and grab onto. He used metaphors, analogies, and stories to illustrate his vision. Some were so memorable, we still use them today. Most people catch the vision when you give them a point for their head, and a picture for their heart.

Tool Five: Emotional Ending

Churchill recognized that a powerful emotional appeal would capture the hearts and commitment of his listeners. He didn't simply speak to the intellect, but the heart of his listeners.

Take a moment and consider how you could effectively communicate your vision to the staff and opinion leaders on campus. How could you use these five tools?

Making Your Point...

In his book, *How To Get Your Point Across in Thirty Seconds or Less*, Milo Frank shares these insights with us:

1. Have an objective.

2. Know your listener.

3. Choose the best approach.

4. Use a "hook."

5. Develop the subject.

6. Paint a picture.

7. Ask for what you want.

When Walt Disney set about planning Disneyland in 1952, he wanted the man who had helped put the Navy back into the Pacific, Admiral Joe Fowler, to lead the project. Some representatives from Disney Studios approached Fowler about the project but he was initially uninterested. He had retired at age 57 and didn't see any reason to go from building up the Navy to building a theme park. As Disney's representatives were explaining this to Disney, Walt said 'Bring him to me.'

Disney cast the vision for his theme park so compellingly that Joe Fowler signed on to head up the development which was later completed in 1955.

Several years later, Walt Disney had a vision to construct Disney World, an even more elaborate and expansive family fun park in Orlando, Florida. The Disney people again wanted Joe Fowler, who was now 77, to lead the project team. And again, Joe was initially uninterested until he heard about the vision from Walt. He got on board and spearheaded the task. Ten years later the Disney people wanted to create Epcot Center, a special section of Disney World that would show the world of the future. Fowler was now 87 years old, but Disney wanted him again to oversee the job. He said, "Cast the vision for me." They did and he led a team that saw Epcot open in 1982. That's the power of compelling vision. How do you get others to buy-in to your vision?

> **HAVE AN OBJECTIVE.**
>
> **KNOW YOUR LISTENER.**
>
> **CHOOSE THE BEST APPROACH.**
>
> **USE A "HOOK."**
>
> **DEVELOP THE SUBJECT.**
>
> **PAINT A PICTURE.**
>
> **ASK FOR WHAT YOU WANT.**

1. Embrace and OWN the vision yourself.

Does the vision capture your heart? Don't move forward until the burden for the need for leaders and a vision for this leadership culture has seized your heart.

2. Engage the SOUL of the people.

The ancient Chinese said that the "will" is like a cart being pulled by two horses: the "mind" and the "emotions." Both horses need to be moving in the same direction to pull the cart forward. We must speak to all three: the mind, will and emotions.

3. Speak to their NEEDS.

We must understand the KEYS to their heart:

- What do they cry about?
- What do they sing about?
- What do they dream about?
- What do they laugh about?
- What do they plan about?
- What do they talk about?

4. Paint PICTURES on the inside of them.

People think and remember in pictures. Images fill their minds as they watch TV, the movies or even log on to the Internet. As we've mentioned, to drive your vision home, people need a POINT for their head, and a PICTURE for their heart.

5. Provide APPLICATION not merely information.

We must furnish something to do, not just think about. People need tangible action steps they can take if they're going to "own" the vision themselves.

6. Communicate the BENEFITS of buying into the vision.

Most people are tuned in to W.I.I.F.M. radio: What's In It For Me? They rarely do anything until they see the personal, measurable benefits of taking action. Put it another way, most people don't change until they…

- KNOW enough that they are able to.
- CARE enough that they want to.
- HURT enough that they have to.

7. Enlarge their HEART (WORLD).

People want to be a part of something bigger than they themselves. Let them see how they can leave a legacy behind them by participating in the vision.

8. Model personal COMMITMENT and call for it from others.

The number one motivational principle is this: People do what people see. They rarely follow mere talk. They will watch the one who is casting the vision to see just how committed they are to the big idea before jumping in themselves. Remember the warning: *"The law is no more. Also—the prophets find no vision from the Lord."* (Lament. 2:9)

9. Allow TIME for acceptance.

Marketing experts and salesmen tell us that people generally need to hear an idea seven times before they will embrace it and call it their own idea. And the time necessary for this ownership varies.

- Approximately 10% of our population are "pioneers."
- About 70% of the population are "settlers."
- Then, about 20% are "antagonists," who may never jump on board with the vision.

The group you must win over are the "settlers"!

10. **Create an ATMOSPHERE.**

Good leaders and visionaries create a sense of destiny, a sense of family and a militant spirit in the people who listen to them. Cultivating an atmosphere is essential to creating a "critical mass" in your constituency. High morale, positive peer pressure and forward momentum are the leader's best friends.

11. **Employ a variety of PEOPLE to help cast the vision in a trickle down process.**

One person cannot "connect" with everybody. The leader responsible for communicating the vision should employ a variety of others who compliment him/her, and can say it in a fresh way to those with a different style and temperament. The vision is disseminated best when the leader shares it with the staff; the staff with their key volunteers; the key volunteers with those in their sphere of influence, and they eventually will connect with the others. The "buy in" should come from the top.

12. **Demonstrate PASSION. (CREDIBILITY)**

Passion begets passion. We don't attract who we want to the vision—we attract who we are. We must demonstrate passion and communicate enough credibility to make them want to follow the vision.

Conclusion: How We Must Handle Vision...

1. See it CLEARLY

2. Show it CREATIVELY

3. Say it CONSTANTLY

Upon the dedication of Disney World, one of the people officiating the ceremony remarked as he was introducing Walt Disney's widow and helping her to the podium, "I wish Walt could have seen this!" Without a moment's hesitation, she replied, "He did!" Disney had visualized in his mind's eye what the park would look like long before it ever took shape on paper or became a physical reality.

The obvious challenge for Pastor John and Tom will be to communicate their vision for the ministry and for developing a leadership culture there at Community Church. If they apply the three Ss above, we believe they will be successful.

CHAPTER EIGHT

Structuring for a Leadership Culture

"Dave, I'd like to introduce you to Pastor John Powell," Tom declared. "He is our senior pastor here at Community Church."

"Pastor John, it's a real pleasure to meet you. Tom has spoken very highly of you," replied Dave Anderson.

It had been a couple of weeks since Tom and Dave had met and a lot had taken place at Community Church in the meantime. Tom and Pastor John were doing their best to implement some of the things they had heard at the recent leadership conference. Dave meanwhile was getting ready for the start of another semester at the University; always a busy time around campus. Dave had agreed to come by the Church to have lunch and discuss the whole idea of creating a leadership culture there. Tom brought in three box lunches and the men sat down to eat and talk.

"Pastor John, Tom tells me that you guys are looking seriously at trying to equip and train lots of new leaders here at Community Church. What brought about the need to do this?" Dave quizzed.

"Well, Dave," Pastor John started, "We have been experiencing some rapid growth in our attendance over the past year. We're trying to assimilate as many of our guests and visitors as possible. We're also in the middle of launching several new ministry initiatives. We realized that if we don't build a foundation of leaders under our ministry structure, it could collapse at some point like a house of cards."

Tom added, "I think we also understood that everything rises and falls on leadership, Dave. Our ministry and the kingdom work here at Community can only rise as far as the leaders can take it."

"Based on my experience at the University, I would tend to agree with both of you. It is very important to have a foundation of real leadership under any organizational structure. No organization, school, church, or otherwise, is going to go farther than the leadership has been," said Dave. "I think there are several things that are real basic to what you are trying to do here. Let me elaborate. First, if you haven't done so, you need to identify your organizational values. These would be the principles that you believe are non-negotiable to your Church. Obviously, some of these may relate to your faith, but others may be items such as 'People are more valuable than things.' Organizational values will help you make decisions quicker and easier because every decision gets put through the grid of your values and what you stand for. If it doesn't fit or if it violates your values, you discard it."

"Dave, when you speak of values, are you talking about our attitudes towards certain things. Or, do you mean our behavior in certain situations?" asked Pastor John.

> ORGANIZATIONAL VALUES WILL HELP YOU MAKE DECISIONS QUICKER AND EASIER BECAUSE EVERY DECISION GETS PUT THROUGH THE GRID OF YOUR VALUES AND WHAT YOU STAND FOR.

"Pastor, attitudes and behaviors are definitely important, but values are more like global beliefs that really guide your actions and judgments regarding specific objects or situations. It's a fact that everyone and every organization have values of some sort. Sometimes we may not be consciously aware of the values we are operating by. The real issue is more how to prioritize your values. What's the most important thing to you, what's second, etc." Dave continued, "For example, I would guess that salvation is probably a core value of yours, Pastor. Probably another value would be taking care of your family. Your Church and leaders have to decide what's the most important thing to you as a group."

"What things do you think are important for us to do Dave as we try to build a leadership culture here at Community Church?" questioned Pastor John.

"I believe one idea that is important is the idea of building a learning community. By that I mean, you should set up a sequence of mentoring and training groups for your emerging and present leaders. Devise a process that includes specific criteria and curriculum for them to walk through. These could be led by your people who are currently in positions of leadership," Dave said.

"What if we laid out a plan that took people through a progressively deeper level of leadership training and mentoring?" Tom added. "We could start with maybe a Survey of Leadership—just basic stuff about leaders, what is leadership, etc. Then we might move into helping people learn practical leadership skills and give them a place to try these skills out in a ministry or something. Finally, we could develop these leaders to the point where they could mentor and train other leaders."

"Tom, that is exactly what I am talking about. You're right on target," said Dave as he stopped to take a bite of his tuna fish sandwich. He washed it down with a drink of spring water and continued, "One thing I know guys from my experience at the

University, 'Leaders are made, not born.' Becoming a leader is a process not an event and it happens best in learning communities just like the one you described Tom."

"One other thing comes to mind as you're thinking about how to structure your organization for a leadership culture and that's power sharing," Dave added.

"What do you mean Dave?" asked Tom.

"We live in a different world than we used to. I see it more perhaps because I am at the University and deal with young men and women all the time. Previously, organizations functioned with top-down hierarchies. Some of these hierarchies were based on control, some were based on influence, and some were based on ownership or class." Dave continued, "Information was restricted by a few people at the top and everybody did what they were told. Today as you're aware we are living in an age of information and knowledge. People want and expect to be included in the decision making process, especially as it impacts them personally. There's a shift in organizations to a more horizontal, consensual, and collaborative mode of operating."

"I see that even in ministry Dave; especially in the past few years. Gen Xers are different than say, Baby Boomers, in how they commit to an organization, cooperate, and desire to be a part of the process. We've had to adapt our ministry style somewhat to accommodate these changes," said Pastor John.

"Guys, I am going to have to get going," indicated Dave as he glanced down at his watch. "I need to meet with some of our senior faculty to discuss a new building project we're considering."

"So, it sounds like you are putting into practice some of what you've been telling us today, Dave," replied Tom.

"I sure am. Guys, I think if you will apply some of these ideas we've discussed today and try to implement them in your ministry, you're going to be miles down the road toward building a real foundation and structure of leadership," Dave stated.

THOUGHTS AND INSIGHTS

Evaluate the statement "Everyone has values. The difference is how they prioritize those values."

What would a 'learning community' look like within your organization? Do you already have a leadership development process?

Have you attempted to make insiders of your leadership team? If so, by what means? If not, why not?

> **EVERYONE HAS VALUES. THE DIFFERENCE IS HOW THEY PRIORITIZE THOSE VALUES.**

CHAPTER NINE

Planning for People Development

"It is only in developing people that we permanently succeed."
HARVEY FIRESTONE

Many pastors and churches today labor under the notion that genuine renewal will occur in their congregations via some mystical, supernatural movement of God. The theology they practice does not revolve around making disciples or equipping the saints for ministry, as the New Testament teaches. Instead, they are hopeful that one day, God will sovereignly move among them, during a service, and folks will somehow mature and experience renewal. It is an unpredictable, subjective, and even mysterious outcome.

Unfortunately, this is precisely why we must rethink our theology. Too often, the means and outcome we desire are unpredictable, ambiguous and even foggy in our minds. We hid behind the smokescreen that says: Revival and renewal are simply the sovereign hand of God at work, and we have nothing to do with when and where they happen.

We excuse our own complacency and disobedience to the fundamentals by saying that God is the Source of all genuine transformation. The truth is, God is, indeed, the source, but He generally never works alone. History teaches us that He is consistently at work in those who practice the art of developing people. If renewal is the outcome we desire; if it is the measuring stick for local church success—then I believe we must return to the biblical pattern of developing people.

WHAT WOULD JESUS DO? (THE QUESTION WE WEAR ON OUR WRISTS.)

It is safe to say that Jesus was intentional about developing people. Note His methodology for "world conquest" during His three and a half year ministry.

1. He stayed up all night praying for the SELECTION of twelve men to develop.
2. He spent the majority of His time with those twelve DISCIPLES.
3. His method for making disciples was MENTORING.
4. Even His ministry to the masses was a model to TRAIN His disciples.
5. He fully expected them to REPRODUCE what He had done, when He left them.
6. The early church reached entire CITIES and NATIONS because they were committed to this practice of developing and discipling people. (Acts 19:10, 17:6)

Jesus' Paradigm for Developing People

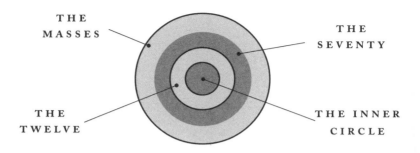

His twelve were faithful to reproduce precisely what He'd passed to them. The Apostle John, for instance, discipled or mentored Polycarp—a man who carried the legacy well into the second century. In fact, the art of disciple-making or training people through developmental relationships continued strong right through the third century before it was dealt a horrible blow in 313 AD. Ironically, the "blow" came from the Emperor Constantine, a confessed Christian man. It was during the year that Constantine declared Christianity as the "State" religion. All of a sudden, God's people moved from being persecuted outcasts, to being part of the system. They were vogue. Instantly, everyone was declared a Christian. Outreach no longer seemed necessary. They began to withdraw from their labor of discipling people. Unfortunately, it was only when God's people stopped developing others that the renewal began to fade as well.

> It was only when God's people stopped developing others that the renewal began to fade as well.

History Repeats Itself

Time and time again, history has told the same story over again. During the 18th century under John Wesley, a movement began called Methodism. Note some of the highlights…

1. Wesley took the Gospel outside the four walls of the CHURCH.

2. Wesley recognized that decisions didn't automatically mean DISCIPLES.

3. Wesley organized converts into **class meetings** for accountability and growth.

4. Wesley began to develop and mentor **lay ministers** who served the church.

5. Wesley built chapels for the purpose of EQUIPPING lay people for ministry.

6. Wesley believed all should be unleashed to minister and REACH their potential.

> **SUCCESS WITHOUT A SUCCESSOR IS A FAILURE.**

John Wesley was committed to two tasks, which his church would later become weak in. First, he was committed to putting the truths and values of his movement on paper. His writings on sanctification, personal growth, discipline, conversion and evangelism are still influencing us today. Second, he was committed to training a second generation of men to lead and serve when he was gone. He somehow knew that success without a successor is a failure.

THE BOTTOM LINE

John F. Kennedy once said that if we do not learn from history, we are destined to repeat it. I believe there are both positive and negative lessons to be learned. If local churches today are going to experience ongoing growth and lay renewal, they must recapture and embrace the lessons of history, from the early church to the Methodist church. Pastors that desire healthy, flourishing congregations must commit themselves to the art of developing people. Further, if they expect to see leaders and lay ministers emerge year after year to serve in their church family—they would do well to design a structure within the church which equips and develops people, moving them from members; to ministers; to mobilizers; to multipliers.

THE ORIGIN OF EQUIPPING

Often, pastors of traditional churches ask the question, "Is it really my job to equip people to serve and lead? Am I not merely to be a shepherd and teach the people on Sunday?" By asking this question, they exhibit an ignorance of the fact that equipping people, and developing leaders, was first God's idea before it was anyone else's. When God instructed Moses, in Numbers 11:16-30, we see a clear imperative given to focus on and raise up lay-leaders from among the people. Note verse 16:

> *"So the Lord said to Moses, 'Gather to Me seventy men… whom you know to be the elders of the people and officers over them; bring them to the tabernacle of meeting, that they may stand there with you.'"*
>
> NUMBERS 11:16-30

In the text that follows, God defines what Moses was to do with them. We see the answer to the question: What do potential leaders need? The passage suggests seven things that lay leaders need from their pastor or point person:

1. They need authority. (v.16: Let them stand there with you…)

2. They need anointing. (v.17: I will put my Spirit upon them…)

3. They need ownership of the vision. (v.17: take the Spirit upon you…put on them)

4. They need responsibility. (v.17: they shall bear the burden with you…)

5. They need specific ministry roles. (v.24: stationed them around the tent…)

6. They need to express their gifts. (v.25: the spirit rested on them; they prophesied.)

7. They need a secure shepherd who will release them to success. (v.26-30)

EXODUS 18:17-27

In a separate text, Exodus 18:17-27, the reality of the need to develop people rings loud and clear to Moses, through his father in law, Jethro. The title for the passage of scripture could easily be: The Day Moses Became a Leader. Dr. John Maxwell suggests it was on that day, when Moses stopped seeing his primary role as caring for the people, and began to see it as equipping leaders for that task. He ultimately became convinced that the people would be cared for better if he stopped trying to do it all—and began to share the leadership with others.

> **PASTORS THAT DESIRE HEALTHY, FLOURISHING CONGREGATIONS MUST COMMIT THEMSELVES TO THE ART OF DEVELOPING PEOPLE.**

THE LIES WE BELIEVE…

We must face the facts. The reason why people fail to become prepared for ministry and leadership in the local church or on campus is because the present leaders have failed to equip them. Further, we believe leaders have failed because they have unwittingly bought into one of a series of "myths" about equipping people. We have listed some of the more popular myths below.

1. The Transfer Myth

They labor under the false hope that leaders will transfer to them from other churches!

2. The Bird-in-the-Hand Myth

They are only concerned with "plugging holes"—and they have enough leaders now.

3. The Irreplaceability Myth

They feel that no one can ever do the leadership thing quite as well as they do.

4. The Short-Sighted Myth
They don't see the future very clearly, and the necessity for more leaders tomorrow.

5. The Inferiority Myth
They quietly fear there may be a better leader that will emerge from the people.

6. The "Easier-To-Do-It-Myself" Myth
We're too busy already—it will require too much work to set up the training necessary.

7. The Reproduction Myth
Despite our own lack of leadership training, we assume we'll reproduce them naturally.

8. The Theology Myth
We somehow think that they will arise out of thin air, since God is sovereign.

DRAWING LINES, WRITING STORIES

As we have already concluded, equipping or developing people is a process not an event. It includes instruction, demonstration, experience and assessment of ministry on a consistent basis. However, it begins when the pastor/leader practices an art that I call: "drawing lines and writing stories." This process will create a structure for ongoing people development.

1. Determine the "STORY" you want to write, through your campus or church.

Every church is writing a story—whether they realize it or not. We write them on accident or on purpose. When we are not intentional about it, we eliminate our chances at making an impact on our communities. We must begin with the end in mind. A pastor or leader must ask himself or herself the question: What do I envision people saying about this church or campus, decades from now? As they consider the divine "story" the organization is to write, he or she must consider these factors:

- The Lord: What is God saying to you about your role in His worldwide plan?

- The Leader: What are your passions and gifts? What do you bring to the table?

- The Laymen: What contribution seems to fit the people God has given you?

- The Location: What opportunities lie in front of you that may direct your course?

- The Landmarks: What destiny markers are sprinkled through your church history?

- The Legacy: Finally, what is it you'd ultimately like to have said about your church or campus?

> **WHAT DO I ENVISION PEOPLE SAYING ABOUT THIS CHURCH OR CAMPUS, DECADES FROM NOW?**

2. Establish what "DECISIONS" you want people to make in the "story."

People who make progress through their spiritual journey make key decisions along the way. These decisions often serve as "breakthrough" points where they take major steps forward. However, while most churches love to see folks make these growth decisions, they don't know how to facilitate them. Most churches play a cruel "hide and seek" game with their congregations. They preach that people ought to become "disciples" but don't offer a process to facilitate that outcome.

• How do we facilitate people making these decisions?

3. Recognize the natural "STAGES" people will grow through.

There are obvious stages that people experience as they grow into leaders within the congregation. As the pastor recognizes them, he must set up "laboratories" for people to experiment at that level. Note the "funnel" diagram, which outlines these stages:

I. People move from outsider to attender.

II. People move from attender to member.

III. People move from member to minister.

IV. People move from minister to leader.

V. People move from leader to leader of leaders.

I. Masses
II. Members
III. Ministers
IV. Mobilizers
V. Multipliers

In a campus setting, emerging student leaders also grow through five similar stages. The campus minister can facilitate growth by providing certain activities at each of these levels.

These stages and activities are shown in the next "funnel" diagram:

I. Activities which introduce students to new relationships, new goals, and the big-picture plan of leadership development.

II. Activities which allow a student to build healthy relationships and people skills, and to demonstrate faithfulness and consistency for the next level.

III. Activities which enable a student to practice servanthood and give of themselves to others. It allows them to demonstrate a servant's heart prior to level four.

I. Orientation
II. Involvement
III. Service
IV. Leadership
V. Multiplication

IV. Activities which provide "laboratories" for students to practice leadership, either long-term or short-term. These could be RAs, Chaplains, small group leaders, team captains, ministry team leaders, task force leaders, etc.

V. Activities for experienced student leaders who have demonstrated mature, healthy leadership and now can mentor and reproduce other leaders.

TIPS ON HELPING PEOPLE THROUGH THE STAGES…

- Each stage represents a relationship and perspective people possess about the church.
- Each stage requires an event that people can participate in that helps them grow.
- Each stage is a "fishing pool" for the next stage of the process.
- People must progress sequentially through each of these stages as a rule.

4. Draw "LINES" in the sand and facilitate your people crossing them.

At this point, a pastor or leader must begin drawing lines in the sand— and challenge the people to take clear steps of commitment that will move them into deeper relationship with God and the church. Many leaders fear drawing these "lines." They hesitate for fear that no one will ever take the step. The truth is, some will and some won't. But, a leader must recognize this reality: he will never know where people really stand until he draws a line in the sand.

What are those lines in the sand? For a pastor some of the "lines" you might have to draw include…

1. THE OWNERSHIP LINE: Challenge people to "own" the church vision, and make it their church home, where they are accountable.

2. THE STEWARDSHIP LINE: Challenge people to steward their resources of time, talent and tithe to the church, to further its ministry.

3. THE LEADERSHIP LINE: Challenge people to assume a place of influence, and intentionally oversee a segment of people in the "story."

4. THE AUTHORSHIP LINE: Challenge people to not only "own" the story of the church, but become a key "writer" or multiplier of that story.

5. Create a "STRUCTURE" for developing people.

All good leadership development systems begin as "people development" systems. You don't produce good leaders unless you first commit to grow people in their beginning stages of your story. The structure must always include spiritual formation. Then, you will eventually turn out leaders as people have grown. Of course, not everyone becomes a formal leader. However, everyone does find their own "place" of service where they fit best.

A campus or church's structure for people development must address their different levels of maturity. For example, a pastor could offer four levels of training/ministry experience to people who are ready to take a further step in their involvement. These "levels" recognize the "stations" people mature through, provide a place for everyone, and also a "pool" to fish from, as the pastor needs to recruit people for deeper involvement and ministry positions in the church.

For example…

A. LEVEL ONE: ORIENTATION *(Monthly)*
This level addresses those who are simply "attenders" but not yet "belongers." Its purpose is to welcome them, to create an atmosphere and climate for growth, to relay the basics in spiritual life, and to communicate to them the goals and opportunities for involvement in the church. One to one appointments could be set following the orientation event. The church is seen as a *benefit*, and a positive source of encouragement to everyone. Those people who come cross an emotional line and start calling the church "their" church, not someone else's.

B. LEVEL TWO: MEMBERSHIP *(Monthly)*
This level addresses those who are "belongers" but not yet "owners" of the vision. By owning the vision, I mean they have stepped over the line of commitment, and now want to declare that they are disciples who are growing, stewards who are giving and members who are going to tell the "story" as well. In the membership class, the instruction time is split between spiritual formation issues, and church family issues. The church is seen as a *family* that people not only belong to, but must be committed to as members. Those people who become members cross a volitional line, and begin to put their "money where their mouth is." (Note: there is nothing sacred about calling this stage, "membership." It is simply a principle step that the people must take in their commitment and accountability).

C. LEVEL THREE: MINISTRY LIFESTYLE TRAINING (M.L.T.) *(Quarterly)*
This level addresses those who "own" the church's vision, but are not serving in ministry. A pastor must embrace the New Testament paradigm that every Christian is called to be a minister. Consequently, the pastor owes it to them to equip them for this task. It is the function of the church leadership. M.L.T. could be a four-week training experience covering issues like matching gifts and people, the attitude and identity of a minister, people skills, ministry disciplines, etc. In this stage, the church is seen as a "laboratory" for people to experiment in using their gifts in service. They cross a tangible line of involvement, and no longer see themselves as mere "consumers"—they are now ministers in the church.

D. LEVEL FOUR: BASIC LEADERSHIP TRAINING (B.L.T.) *(Quarterly)*
This level addresses those who are involved in service, but have undeveloped leadership potential. The training will turn "ministers" into "leaders." It will not only multiply people who do the work, but also people who oversee other workers. The more leaders a church has, the more growth potential it possesses, and the greater opportunity it has to reach the surrounding community. In this training experience (which could also be done in four weeks), only those with appropriate leadership gifts move forward. A church does not frustrate people without any leadership potential—and force them to believe they must become leaders. B.L.T.

serves a vital function, but a pastor should not expect everyone to go through it. B.L.T. might cover such issues as leadership vs. ministry, the disciplines of a leader, leadership skills, the anatomy of a leader, etc. The pastor then moves as Moses did (Exodus 18), and place those who have gone through B.L.T. in appropriate leadership positions.

E. LEVEL FIVE: "OASIS" (LEADERSHIP LUNCH) *(Monthly or Quarterly)*
This level serves those people already in leadership, and provides ongoing development on a monthly or quarterly basis. It resources leaders with a time for communication, for mutual prayer, for encouragement over shared victories, and an opportunity for further training and development. Optimally, it includes a plenary time for all leaders—then, specialty sessions for leaders with and without experience:

1. LEADERSHIP FOUNDATIONS: Training for those who have been leaders less than one year.

2. LEADERSHIP FITNESS: Roundtable for those who have been leaders more than one year.

The issues covered in each of the specialty training times are to be appropriate for the leaders who attend them. Leadership Foundations, for instance, would cover fundamentals that every leader needs to cover, such as servant leadership, communication skills, priorities, conflict resolution, managing people, etc. Leadership Fitness is more of a roundtable discussion, allowing experience leaders to remain on the cutting edge, and sharpening their leadership skills. Issues they might discuss would be: overcoming burnout, mentoring and spiritual reproduction, confrontation and discipline, spiritual passion, effective recruitment, leaders as intercessors, etc.

6. **Evaluate your structure by the QUALITY and QUANTITY of leaders you develop.**
The pastor or leader's goal is to produce more and better disciples and leaders. If his or her system is effective, they should see an increase within a year or two of the leaders they have to choose from, in the church or school. The system, in other words, should begin producing a "pool" of leaders to draw from for positions in the Body. If a pastor observes that leaders are coming out of the system, then he probably is doing a good job at all of the levels of people development. The objectives can be drawn up in simple terms:

Goal #1: To make more and better disciples of Jesus.

Goal #2: To build more and better leaders of people.

Quantity question: Are they more numerous now than in the past?

Quality question: Are they better now than in the past?

THE LEADER'S PERSONAL EVALUATION:

1. Step A: Choose the Men.

   How creative am I at finding new people to invest in?

2. Step B: Cultivate the Models.

   How am I doing at turning my men into examples?

3. Step C: Create the Ministries.

   How am I at creating ministry opportunities for them?

4. Step D: Construct the Management.

   How am I at monitoring them along the way?

5. Step E: Communicate the Mindset.

   How am I at constantly keeping the vision alive?

6. Step F: Celebrate the Mentoring.

   How do I encourage and celebrate growth?

7. **Make ADJUSTMENTS each year to maintain quality control and progress.**

   Change is necessary. If it works today, we cannot assume it will tomorrow. A church will either evaluate or stagnate. There must be continual improvement. A pastor must strive to stay ahead of the game, especially in the area of people development.

   Growth and change are topics that have been studied for years. Today, however, growth and change take place at a much faster rate than ever before in recorded history. British author Charles Handy has popularized the **"Sigmoid Curve"** in his attempt to explain and exhort leaders and managers regarding corporate change. Note the diagrams on the next page.

> **THE PASTOR OR LEADER'S GOAL IS TO PRODUCE MORE AND BETTER DISCIPLES AND LEADERS.**

CHANGE AT POINTS A AND B...

The diagram to the right indicates that as corporations grow, they rise in a fashion similar to the arrow. When the arrow is at its peak, production has peaked for the organization in its present mode of operation.

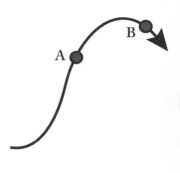

Most corporations don't recognize the need for change until Point B, when production has begun to decline. Handy argues that leaders must have the foresight to predict trends, and change before decline sets in, at Point A. This is difficult, because no one else in the organization sees a need to "fix" what isn't broken.

PERIOD OF CHAOS...

If the leader makes the change at Point A, he will incur the misunderstanding of others. Then, for the season between Point A and Point B—the organization will experience a period of "chaos" where everyone feels they are in a state of "flux"; routines have been disturbed and the security of the familiar is absent. This chaos can only be avoided if the leader waits until it's obvious the change is needed—however, at this point, it is too late to stay on top of the game. We must change before it is obvious.

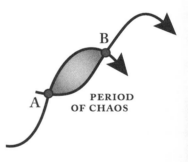

CONSTANT GROWTH
MEANS CONSISTENT CHAOS!

Consequently, if an organization desires to stay on top, they are literally inviting chaos to be their constant companion, as in the diagram on the right. There will be a consistent trend of change, growth, recognition for more change—and chaos. If leaders and organizations are secure enough to endure it, this chaotic, flexible mode of operation will save their future.

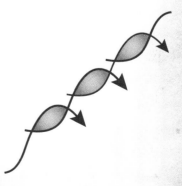

The fact of the matter is—all of us will change with the future.

The question is: Will it be too late?

DRAWING A CONCLUSION

When all is said and done, we believe there are a handful of conclusions that can be drawn regarding the art of "people development" in the local church or school campus. If a church or school is to consistently produce quality ministers and leaders from their constituents, it is optimal that the pastor or leader embraces the following principles:

The Principles...

1. A church or campus will see consistent streams of leaders emerge each year only as they intentionally establish systems to foster their development.

2. A pastor must see his role not merely as shepherd to the flock, but equipper of the flock.

3. Structure must be created which builds people at each "station" or phase of growth they experience in the local church or school campus.

4. Leaders must make the following decisions for themselves and the staff they hire:

   a. The leader is first a "model" because while we teach what we know, we reproduce what we are. People will follow the lead of the leader.

   b. The leader is also a "minister" because while he or she does perform leadership functions beyond that of a minister, he can never leave behind the function of servanthood.

   c. The leader is also a "mentor" because he now is selecting people, and intentionally investing his life into them.

   d. The leader is also a "monitor" because managing the system, and "fishing" for potential people at each level of the structure becomes paramount. He is a recruiter.

   e. The leader is a "mobilizer" because he must keep the "heat" on for his people to grow, stretch, and become who they need to be spiritually.

"DECISIONS, DECISIONS"

So often, ministry in the church or on a school campus is haphazard and unstable because of the lack of preparation. People may decide to commit themselves to being involved in some event/ministry... but without an established system of care in place, it's difficult to keep track of who is where. One of the smartest moves a local church or campus can make is to pause and then list the decisions they (and God!) want their people to make... and then to create vehicles to receive and facilitate those decisions.

Decisions that our people should make...

A. To COME… *(The decision to come to the church.)*
How do we facilitate that decision?

_____

_____

_____

B. To RECEIVE CHRIST… *(The decision to become a Christian).*
How do we facilitate that decision?

_____

_____

_____

C. To LEARN… *(The decision to get established in the basics).*
How do we facilitate that decision?

_____

_____

_____

D. To IDENTIFY… *(The decision to identify with Christ and the Church in baptism).*
How do we facilitate that decision?

_____

_____

_____

E. To RELATE… *(The decision to build a network of friendships and accountability).*
How do we facilitate that decision?

_____

_____

_____

F. To COMMIT… *(The decision of ownership, to join the church "team" in ministry).*
How do we facilitate that decision?

_____

_____

_____

G. To Give... *(The decision of stewardship—time, talents and treasure).*
How do we facilitate that decision?

_____

_____

_____

H. To Grow... *(The decision to mature spiritually in a discipleship experience).*
How do we facilitate that decision?

_____

_____

_____

I. To LEAD... *(The decision to formally influence others: reproduction and multiplication).*
How do we facilitate that decision?

_____

_____

_____

PLAN FOR PEOPLE DEVELOPMENT

Our plan to develop people who come, must address their different levels of maturity. We will offer four levels of training/ministry to those who are ready to take a further step of involvement. This will provide a place for everyone, and also a "pool" to fish from, as we need to recruit people for deeper involvement and ministry positions in the church.

1. Level One: Orientation

This level will address whose who are simply "attenders" but not yet "belongers." Its purpose is to welcome them, to create an atmosphere and climate for growth, and to communicate to them the goals as well as opportunities for involvement in the church or school family. One to one appointments are set, after the presentation. Orientation includes:

- Food or Dessert
- Music
- Welcome and Purpose
- Video of the Church
- Testimonies of Laymen
- Future Dreams
- Involvement Opportunities
- One-to-One Appointments

2. Level Two: Ministry Lifestyle Training (M.L.T.)

This level will address those who "belong" to the church or attend the school, but are not serving. We believe every Christian is called to be a minister, so we owe it to them to equip them for this task. It is the function of leadership. This will serve to not only "grow" people's potential, but also provide gifted people for needed ministries and seal their relationship with the church or school. M.L.T. topics include:

- The Identity of a Minister
- Matching Gifts and People
- Developing People Skills
- Ministry Disciplines

(Following the four-week training, a field trip is taken)

3. Level three: Basic Leadership Training (B.L.T.)

This level will address those who are involved in service, but have undeveloped leadership potential. The training will turn "ministers" into "leaders," and provide people who do not simply do the work, but multiply and oversee the workers. The more leaders we have, the more growth potential we possess, and the greater opportunity we have to reach the surrounding community. B.L.T. topics include:

- The Disciplines of a Leader
- Leadership vs. Ministry
- Your Leadership Skills
- Anatomy of a Leader

(Following the four-week training, a field trip is taken.)

4. Level Four: Oasis—Leadership Lunch

This level services those who are involved in leadership. It is ongoing leadership development, on a monthly basis. It provides a time for communication among other leaders, a source of encouragement, a time for mutual prayer and an opportunity for further training and development. Leadership Lunches include:

- Lunch (Our way of saying thanks)
- Vision Casting (Sharing of victories)
- Prayer/Worship (Lifting up God, each other)
- Administration (Information)
- Huddle Time (Relational)
- Skill Training (Two tracts)

  The "skill training" has two tracts, designed to meet the needs of those attending:

  1. "LEADERSHIP FOUNDATIONS" is training for those who have been a leader for one year or less. It focuses on the foundations of leadership at the

church or school; those issues we all need to embrace. It is repeated each year for first year leaders.

2. "LEADERSHIP FITNESS" is training for those who have been a leader for more than one year. It relieves them from having to go through the same issues repeatedly, and enables them, in a round-table style, to discuss deeper issues in their growth.

FOUNDATION TOPICS	FITNESS TOPICS
1. Attitudes of a Leader	1. Overcoming Burnout
2. Managing People	2. Confrontation/Discipline
3. Maintaining Priorities	3. Effective Recruitment
4. Servant Leadership	4. The Power of Fasting
5. Dealing with Difficulties	5. The Art of Intercession
6. Communication Skills	6. Leaders are Readers
7. Building an Outreach Mindset	7. Redemptive People Skills
8. Casting Vision	8. Dump, Delegate or Develop
9. Modeling Spiritual Disciplines	9. Spiritual Authority
10. Mentoring/Developing Others	10. Excellent vs. Authentic
11. Relational Skills	11. Listening Skills
12 Spiritual Reproduction	12. Spiritual Passion

Chapter Ten
Graduation Day

Tom Jacobs stood with his hand firmly on the tall, dark tree. He moved it slowly across the rough bark. He thought to himself how trees bring the present and past together. Not twenty some years before he had stood on this same spot while a student at the University. He had spent the last hour walking around the school remembering the students, the teachers, and the good times he had enjoyed while here many years ago. In some ways little had changed. Oh, the school had erected a couple of new buildings, additional student parking, and even a new computer lab but much was still the same. Students were walking vigorously across the campus heading off to classes. Young guys and girls were engrossed in seemingly deep conversations about literature and history. A couple of guys were tossing a Frisbee on the hillside and the school library was doing a brisk business today as students were checking out books to begin research papers.

His University days had been of time of growth, exploration, and learning for him. Everyday new worlds of knowledge seemed to be opened up by his professors. He had soaked it all in like a dry, wrung out sponge. Now, here he was again. It seemed to him that the last several months had been a time of 'going back to school.' His work at Community Church had been going well. He and Pastor John had set about trying to implement much of what they had learned about creating a leadership culture—from Dave Anderson, from the leadership conferences they had attended, and from some of the books they were reading.

Pastor had started a monthly 'Leadership Summit' where he got his top leaders together and personally mentored and trained them. This had really gone over big for them and was beginning to pay some dividends in the form of people taking the initiative to start and lead certain ministries there at the church. They had also developed a small mentoring group program called "The Leadership Academy" where emerging leaders were taught and mentored by seasoned ministry veterans. The focus was on acquiring practical leadership skills along with understanding the spiritual formation of a leader. The eventual goal was to have these Academy graduates lead new ministries and also mentor others that would come along behind them. Tom and Pastor John had come to understand that people seem to learn best in a community where someone could help guide the process. Was everybody in the program going to be a super leader? No. But, they realized everybody would need leadership skills in some capacity and everybody had the ability to improve on the leadership skills they currently possessed.

"Hello, Tom." Joyce Colson remarked before he could get a word of greeting out. He had been such a regular here the past several months that she must have wondered if he was coming on the school's payroll. "He's been waiting for you." With that she opened the door to Dave Anderson's office and showed Tom in.

"Tom, my good man. How are you doing today?" said Dave to the younger man.

"Dave, I couldn't be better. I've been on campus for a little while just kind of strolling down memory lane. I walked around the grounds, and went in a few of the buildings. I even stopped by the student center and grabbed me a coffee and a bagel earlier. I really enjoy coming back to this place. It just seems so full of life to me," Tom explained.

"Well, we're always glad to have one of our own come back. Tell me what you guys have been doing over at Community Church the past few months," Dave asked. Tom proceeded to fill in the details about the monthly Leadership Summit, The Leadership Academy, and how the whole idea of a leadership culture was beginning to take root there.

"Dave, you wouldn't believe it. We've got so many young leaders running around there, it's incredible. I am just amazed at the change that is taking place. And, it's affecting our entire Church culture," Tom continued. "People want to be involved and developed. They're asking us to place them in ministry positions where they are most gifted. Ministry participation and involvement are on the increase and our people really seem to be catching the vision."

"Tom, that's fantastic to hear. I am pleased to also hear you talk about your vision. Remember when we met down at Starbucks several months ago and we had that long conversation about vision? I felt like I had backed the truck up and dumped the whole load that morning. You were beginning to glaze over on me," Dave joked.

"You're right Dave. I felt so overwhelmed at all the talk about vision, mission, making vision carriers out of our people, etc. It took me a little while to get my arms around it," replied Tom. "But, I'm here to tell you, it wasn't wasted time at all. No, this stuff has really taken root and is beginning to grow like a tree over at Community Church."

"I am really glad to hear that friend. I knew it was not time wasted when we spent those mornings and afternoons together. We've got to remember, 'change takes time.' And, when you're talking about moving an organizational culture in a new direction, it just doesn't happen overnight. You mentioned a tree. I think that's a good analogy to creating a culture of leadership within your Church. It starts out small with just a few people understanding the dream. As you water it and nurture it, others come on board and want to share in the vision. It grows a little year by year until one day; you've got this massive tree with loads of branches giving support, shade and comfort to the community around it. It kind of puts me in mind of the mustard seed that Jesus speaks about in the Gospels. It's such a tiny dark seed. Who would think a large tree could come from it that would provide a place of shelter to the birds of the air?" Dave said slowly.

He stopped for just a moment as if pondering some great truth and then said, "Tom, it strikes me that creating a culture of leadership is also a work of faith. Just like the farmer who plants a seed but doesn't know for sure if it will germinate and produce a crop, you guys started planting the idea of a leadership culture there at Community Church. You didn't know for sure if it would take root but you continued to water it by casting the vision and communicating a compelling dream that others wanted to be a part of. I am just believing with you that some day, that small shoot that started several months ago will grow into a work that brings shelter, comfort and support to our community and perhaps the world."

"Dave, I appreciate your analogy and I am going to believe with you that the process we've started at Community Church will bear much fruit for the kingdom in the future," Tom proclaimed.

"Tom, do you remember our illustration of the rubber band? We're either stretching up toward the vision or pulling the vision down to our current realities," Dave said. "Also remember, your goal is to make 'vision carriers' out of your leaders—current, emerging and future leaders. What else would you say is important to creating a leadership culture?" Dave asked.

"I understand that creating change in an organization requires a plan. It doesn't just happen. In fact, it's going to take establishing a sense of urgency for the change and creating a guiding coalition to help push it through. We're going to have to communicate the desired changes to our people, and generate some short-term wins. Eventually, we know we'll have to anchor the changes in our culture if we want them to remain long-term," Tom responded.

"Tom, I believe you've got enough knowledge and experience under your belt to help the next guy if someone were to come along," Dave replied.

"I appreciate that coming from you, Dave. Your insights and guidance have been critical to the development process. Thanks for everything you've done to help me and help Community Church," Tom said. He rose, shook the older man's hand and left his office.

———◆———

A couple of months had passed since Tom had last met with Dave. He was wondering how his leadership mentor was doing. 'He's probably breaking in a new batch of students about now' Tom imagined. His daydreaming was interrupted by a knock at his office door. "Come in," he said.

"Tom, I have a young man out in our office who would like to speak with you. He says Dave Anderson sent him over here. Can you take a minute to speak with him?" his secretary questioned.

"Sure Sharon. Send him on in," Tom replied.

"How are you doing today? I'm Tom Jacobs. What might I be able to do for you?" Tom greeted as he stood up and offered his hand.

"Well, my name is Brad Wood. Dave Anderson over at the University gave me your name and said I ought to get with you about something," said the youngish visitor. "You see, I graduated over there a couple of years back and now pastor a small church not two miles down the road from here. I've been watching what you guys have been doing at Community Church over the last year and I'm convinced I need to begin to grow my leaders at our church. Do you think you could help me?"

Tom leaned back in his chair. He remembered Dave asking him if he thought he could take someone through this leadership development process. Maybe, just maybe, he had Brad Wood in mind when he had asked. Tom started out by saying, "Brad, what you are talking about will take a massive effort on your part. You don't need to simply train a few leaders. The problem you are facing can only be solved by building a *culture of leadership.*" The mentoring cycle had come full circle. And that is as it should be.

Recommended Resources

Arbinger Institute
Leadership and Self Deception

Barna, George
The Power of Vision

Bennis, Warren (ed.)
The Future of Leadership

Elmore, Tim
Mentoring: How to Invest Your Life in Others
Habitudes: Images That Form Leadership Habits and Attitudes
Leveraging Your Influence: Impacting Your Campus for Christ

Gladwell, Malcolm
The Tipping Point

Kouzes, James & Barry Posner
Credibility

Kotter, John
Leading Change

Maxwell, John
The 17 Laws of Teamwork

Phegan, Barry
Developing Your Company Culture

Schein, Edgar
Organizational Culture and Leadership

Senge, Peter
The Fifth Discipline

Stanley, Andy
Visioneering

A Word About Growing Leaders
Hungry for more?

"Growing Leaders" is committed to equipping the next generation of leaders, who will change the world. We want to transform you from the inside out, so you can turn your world upside down. This book is one of many resources, which equips you to lead in a healthy, effective way. We have a variety of tools to help you learn to lead while you experience community. Some of those tools are:

> Leadership resources for mentoring communities

> A Leadership Academy

> Videos, CDs and workbooks

> A Leadership Forum

> Conferences held on your campus

> Free electronic subscriptions

Our goal is to partner with campuses to help them nurture a leadership culture. Our website includes some ideas on how to begin that process for both staff and students.

Dr. Tim Elmore spearheads a team of leaders who want to invest in your life and in your campus. Let us know if you want to take another step in your leadership journey:

www.GrowingLeaders.com